The Western Edge

Work and Management in the Information Age

by

TJERK HUPPES

Professor 'Economic and Social Impact of
Information Technology'

1987 **KLUWER ACADEMIC PUBLISHERS**
DORDRECHT / BOSTON / LANCASTER

Distributors

for the United States and Canada: Kluwer Academic Publishers, P.O. Box 358, Accord Station, Hingham, MA 02018-0358, USA
for the UK and Ireland: Kluwer Academic Publishers, MTP Press Limited, Falcon House, Queen Square, Lancaster LA1 1RN, UK
for all other countries: Kluwer Academic Publishers Group, Distribution Center, P.O. Box 322, 3300 AH Dordrecht, The Netherlands

Library of Congress Cataloging in Publication Data

```
Huppes, T.
  The Western edge.

  Includes bibliographical references and index.
  1. Organizational change.  2. Work design.
3. Management--Data processing.  4. Technological
innovations.  I. Title.
HD58.8.H86  1987        338'.06        87-4087
```

ISBN 90-247-3495-9

Copyright

Acknowledgments

The original version of this book was published in Dutch. The text was based on the results of a research project sponsored by the Dutch Government on the economic and social implications of information technology.

Since the book has stimulated considerable discussion in Dutch business and academic circles, friends and colleagues kept encouraging me to translate it and make it available to a wider readership. 'The Western Edge' would never have appeared however, had it not been for a group of managers (all members of the Dutch 'Association of Department and Chain Stores') who kindly raised the money for the translation. I would have mentioned their names individually to express my gratitude for their generous support, but they preferred to stay anonymous.

Of those I can thank explicitly, I first of all want to mention the students who worked with me on the project: Margien Bouma, Nico Drok, Ynte Jan Kuindersma, Kees Reezigt and Wout Vogelesang. Their dedication to the project and their patience with me were quite admirable. Thanks are due also to David Henebury who did a splendid job translating the book. An invaluable contribution was made by my friend and colleague Abbe Mowshowitz from the City University of New York. His work on the project as a consultant has had a profound impact on the book. He also suggested the title 'The Western Edge' for the English version: an apt description of the essence of the work. Of course, I take full responsibility for the arguments presented in the text. Last but not least, I want to thank my wife and children who cheerfully endured my protracted preoccupation with a project, that extended far beyond the original plan.

January 1987   Tjerk Huppes
University of Groningen
The Netherlands

Contents

Part I: Diagnosis

1. The challenge

A ghost is haunting the Western world. It responds to the name 'Nippon': the land of the rising sun. 'Lessons from Japan' preoccupy managers both in the United States and in Europe. Books about Japanese management turn out to be bestsellers; conferences on this topic are 'en vogue'. The main conclusion of this book is diametrically opposed to the conventional wisdom about the challenge we are facing. Not Japan, but the West itself has the comparative advantages which can guarantee a long-term leading position. The key to success lies in the combination of (1) information technology and (2) the most prominent characteristic of Western society: individualism. Information technology opens up the possibility of exploiting individualism and related characteristics such as autonomy and creativity. These offer a much better guarantee for a competitive edge than the initiative-killing, group dependant Japanese culture. To optimally utilize the 'Western Edge' it is necessary, simultaneous with the technological innovation of firms, to reintegrate work tasks, to de-Taylorize production organizations, and to make production responsive to ever changing market demand. In short: the historical process of division of work should be reversed. Unlike technology in the industrial past, information technology appears to be an excellent vehicle to achieve this.

Not only the lessons from Japan, but also those from the industrial past should therefore be forgotten. The engines of growth and expansion in the economy in the past – division of work, increase in scale, mass production – are outdated. The main cause of this lies in the accelerated rate of technological progress and the related market turbulence. A large bureaucratic organization functions excellently as long as technology advances relatively slowly and market conditions are fairly stable. However, if technology accelerates, or as nowadays, this acceleration takes on a permanent character, such an organization lacks the necessary flexibility to survive. Under these circumstances managers are compelled to innovate drastically the organizational structure of their firms.

From a macro-perspective the break with the industrial past is in fact already apparent. One indication of this is the decline in industry's share of total employment in Western countries since 1970. Due to the continuing impact of information technology this decline can be expected to continue in the future. In the meantime the so-called information sector in our economies has grown to become the largest sector. More specifically, the trendshift can be observed in the transformation of the production process in all sectors. Case studies of flexible production automation, office automation and the use of computer networks, show evidence of this trendshift in at least three dimensions: the input, the organization, and the output of the production process. With regard to work (the input), examples can be given of upgrading both in the work content and the degree of autonomy. The historical trend of continuing degradation and deskilling seems to be reversing, though as yet hesitantly. Similar observations can be made with regard to the transformation of the organization of firms, where the historical process of horizontal and vertical differentiation is being reversed in order to increase flexibility and preserve a competitive edge. Contrary to the experience of industrial past, the interests of employers and employees seem to be converging. With regard to the type of product (the output), mass production is losing ground. Batch sizes in all kinds of industries are declining, and the significance of custom made goods and services is increasing. The trendshift with the past is finally accentuated by the rapidly growing information sector with its many, small, non-hierarchically organized firms that produce customized services.

Less positive is the impact of information technology on the quantity of work. Unemployment will rise unlesss we find ways to redistribute work by reducing working hours, creating more part time jobs, early retirement, etc. Contrary to what is often assumed, accelerated (technological) innovation does not increase but decrease employment. From a historical perspective re-distribution of work is by no means a new phenomenon. Since the turn of this century, the number of hours worked per year has declined in all Western countries by more than 40%. The difference between then and now is that this process will now have to be accelerated. An average reduction of working hours of around 25% for the period 1980–2000 may very well be necessary to keep everybody working.

The social evolution of the information society reinforces the necessity of a fundamental reorientation of our economies. Informatization – in the sense of increasing intensification and diversification of information activities – accelerates the historical trend towards individualization and differentiation of society. With regard to the employee's work orientation, this trend shows itself by an increasing desire for self-actualization and autonomy at work. These changes on the supply side of the labour market are clearly incompatible with the job profiles of the industrial past. They do, however, converge with the change on the demand side of the labour market which the implementation of information technology allows for. In particular, more enlightened managers are adapting the organization of their firms to this new work orientation and are being rewarded by productivity increase. Designing good jobs turns out to be good business practice. With regard to the consumer market, the individualization of society leads to an increasing diversification of demand which forces firms to shift their focus from traditional mass production to client-oriented goods and services.

The break with the industrial past is therefore not only tech-nologically possible, but also both economically and socially nec-essary. In fact the Western business world *is confronted by a fundamental choice*. On the one hand, we could stick to con-ventional methods of technological innovation, thereby leaving the organization of our firms untouched and wasting a potential contribution of human resources to profits. On the other hand, we could exploit information technology for simultaneous social and technological innovation of our firms. In the past, social innovation was primarily regarded as a luxury only beneficial to the worker. Nowadays it appears to be a precondition for a structural increase of our competitive edge in the future. The action that has to be taken clearly contrasts with the widely recommended 'lessons from Japan'. The success of Japanese firms has its roots in the (as yet) pre-individualistic Japanese culture. Imitation of Japan implies regression rather than innovation. For Western firms, simultaneous socio-technological innovation is the key to success. The final chapter of this book highlights some pioneering examples in both the industrial and the service sector.

Part II: The end of the industrial age?

Western society appears to be at a turning point. The emergence of discontinuities, analogous to those present at the time of the Industrial Revolution around 1800, lend credence to this observation. A characteristic feature of the industrial age was the rise of the industrial sector. From around 1970 onwards, however, the share of industrial employment has declined in all Western countries, and further declines can be expected in the future (chapter 2). The question is whether or not this reverse also implies a trendshift in the characteristic processes of division of work, increasing scale, and increasing mass production of the industrial past, and if so, what will be the consequences for industrial policy. To answer this question we shall first look at the opposite ends of a historical continuum, with respect to which the business world has so far moved to the right, but may well reverse its steps in the future (chapter 3).

2. The industrial versus the information sector

The idea that the industrial age is coming to an end dates from the beginning of the 1960s when the Harvard sociologist Daniel Bell[1] advanced the notion of a 'post-industrial society'. The decline of the industrial sector and the complementary rise of the service sector had then already started in the USA. Figure 2.1. puts this decline in a historical and comparative perspective. It gives a view of the share of employment of the industrial sector in a number of Western countries in the period 1890–1984. From around 1970 a collective decline of the industrial sector appears to have taken place simultaneously in all countries. True enough, the trend in different countries shows earlier fluctuations, but a simultaneous decline has never occurred before. The historical course is perhaps most representatively shown in the Netherlands. After a continuous increase from 1890, the industry sector reached a turning point in the 1960s, and then declined relatively rapidly. In Germany and France the decline occurs somewhat later; in the USA and the UK earlier. The decline in England – the first industrialized country – dates in fact from around 1900 when the British hegemony was assumed by the USA. The decline in the USA dates from 1950.

The collective de-industrialization of Western economies can be explained in a number of ways. Obviously there is some connection with the world-wide depression which has been particularly disruptive since 1980. At the same time, however, there is good reason to emphasize the impact of information technology, i.e. the innovation of the production process based on this technology. The relatively weak link between 'depression' and 'declining industrial employment' is illustrated in figure 2.2. The figure shows the relationship between sales and employment in the American car industry (General Motors, Ford and Chrysler),

Figure 2.1. The share of employment in the industrial sector in a number of
Western countries in the period 1890–1984 (in percentages of the
active workforce).

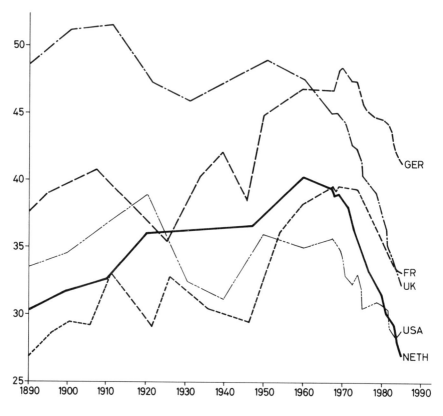

Source: before 1960: B.R. Mitchell, *European Historical Statistics 1950–1975,* Mcmillan,
London 1975, pp. 163, 164, 167 and 171.
U.S. Bureau of the Census, *Historical Statistics of the United States,*
Colonial Times to 1970, p. 139. (The USA statistics before 1960
have been increased by 6.3% to link up with the OECD statistics.)
1960–1984:   OECD, *Historical Statistics,* Paris, 1986.

the topten of the Fortune 500 and two Dutch multinationals
(Philips and Unilever) for the period 1960–1984. All four cases in
fact show the same paradoxical picture. Employment has declined dramatically from around 1970, while at the same time sales
have been booming (the time series have not been corrected for
inflation, but even then an increase in sales during the 1970s would
have been apparent). One would therefore have expected an
increase rather than a decrease in employment.

Figure 2.2. Sales and employment in the American car industry (General Motors, Ford and Chrysler), the topten of the Fortune 500 and two Dutch multinationals (Philips and Unilever) in the period 1960–1984.

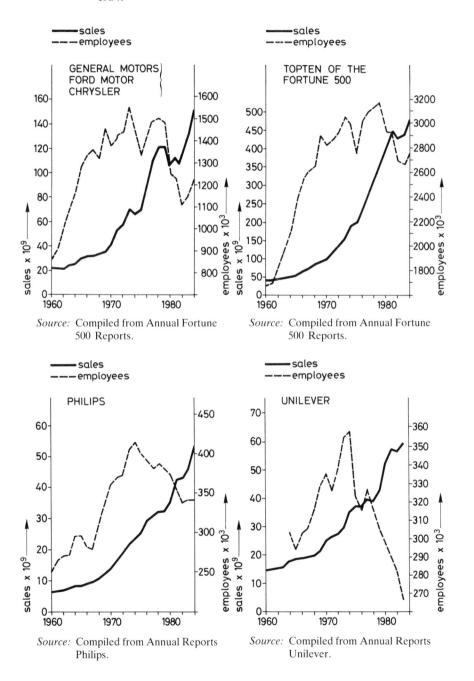

Figure 2.3. Capital intensity and employment in the American car industry
(General Motors, Ford and Chrysler), the top ten of the Fortune 500
and two Dutch multinationals (Philips and Unilever) in the period
1960–1984.

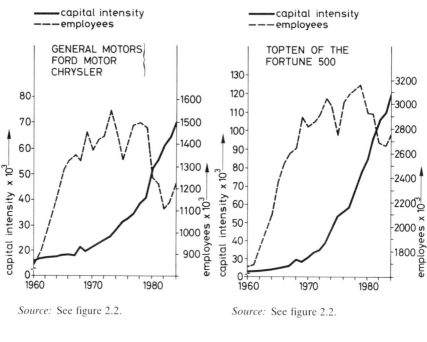

Source: See figure 2.2.   Source: See figure 2.2.

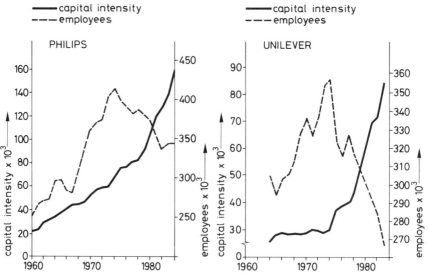

Source: See figure 2.2.   Source: See figure 2.2.

The paradoxical course of sales and employment in the 1970s can be understood if one also considers the capital intensification of the production process to which information technology has contributed so much. Figure 2.3. shows employment and capital intensification in the same period. The rate of capital intensification in the 1970s accelerated to the extend that employment declined. Alongside the depression, technological innovation appears to be a decisive determinant of the decline in employment (see also chapter 4 and 5).

The firms in figure 2.2. and 2.3. are by no means exceptions. Most of the large firms in America listed in the Fortune 500 show the same trends: sales and investment per employee are going up, while the number of employees is going down (IBM is one of the few exceptions; employment in this company is still going up, be it at a decreasing rate). Even smaller firms often conform to this historically unique behaviour. Take for example the case of the (typically) Dutch bicycle industry. Twenty years ago the largest firm in this industry employed 800 workers who produced around 80,000 bikes per year. Nowadays 400 workers produce over 250,000, almost exclusively as a result of the automation of the production process.

The question is how the trendshift in industrial employment will develop in the future. To answer this it is important to realize that the industrial sector is particularly sensitive to automation and robotization because of its relatively extensive division of work. In general it is true to say that the more advanced the division of work, the easier it is for information technology to be applied. The trendshift is therefore in no way temporary but structural. Further innovation (re-industrialization) may indeed promote sales, but not a return to the industrial employment level of the 1960s. On the contrary, a further decline can be expected in the future. A report from the 'Netherlands Study Centre for Technology Trends' predicts for example that 'as a result of further automation a continually smaller part of the workforce will be employed in industry. A decline within ten years of up to half the present number of working hours (to maintain the current production level) is not improbable'.[2]

The decline of industrial employment (including the predictions

Figure 2.4. The sectoral development (the number of workers per sector in percentages of the total active workforce) in the USA in the period 1860–1980.

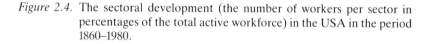

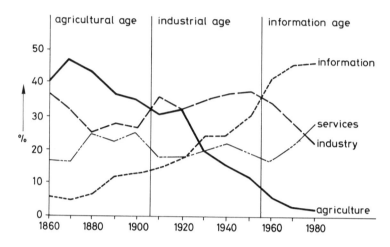

Source: M.U. Porat, *Information Economy, Volume 1. Definition and Measurement,* Washington DC, 1977.

of the future) supports the idea of the end of an era. A second illustration of this can be found in the work of the American Porat,[3] who differentiates the workforce into four instead of the traditional three sectors: agriculture, industry, services, plus the information sector. On the grounds of detailed research on 440 professions since 1860, he concludes that during the 1950s the information sector in the USA surpassed the industrial sector, and that since then the USA has entered the post-industrial or information era (see figure 2.4.). Porat considers the information sector to be 'the part of the economy that produces, processes and distributes information goods and services. Included in this sector are computing, telecommunication, media, education, advertising, accounting, printing and part of finance and insurance'. The transition to the information era is seen by Porat as the latest step in the transformation of the Western world since the 18th century.

Inspired by Porat, the OECD[4] has calculated the post war growth of the information sector for a number of member states. The result is reproduced in figure 2.5. with the complementary table 2.1. In all countries it appears that the information sector has

Figure 2.5. Post-war sectoral shifts in a number of Western countries.

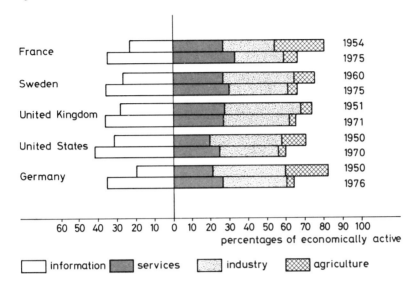

Source: OECD, *Information Activities, Electronics and Telecommunication Technologies, ICCP 6, Paris, 1981.*

increased strongly. In the 1970s this sector surpasses all the other sectors in each country. Table 2.2. gives a view of the origin of the growth of the information sector. Half to two thirds of the professions which are assigned to the information sector originate – as

Table 2.1. Post war sectoral shifts in a number of Western countries.

	Year	Information	Services	Industry	Agriculture
France	1954	20.3	24.1	30.9	24.7
	1975	32.1	28.1	29.9	9.9
Sweden	1960	26.0	26.8	36.5	10.7
	1975	34.9	29.8	30.6	4.7
United Kingdom	1951	26.7	27.5	40.4	5.4
	1971	35.6	27.0	34.2	3.2
United States	1950	30.5	19.1	38.4	12.0
	1970	41.1	24.1	31.5	3.3
Germany	1950	18.3	20.9	38.3	22.5
	1976	33.2	25.9	35.1	5.8

Source: OECD, *Information Activities, Electronics and Telecommunication Technologies, ICCP 6, Paris, 1981.*

could be expected – in the service sector. However, the contribution of the industrial sector share has also increased considerably. This is particularly interesting as the significance of the industrial sector as a whole has declined in this period. Obviously, the share of information professions in this sector is becoming more and more important. In the industrial era the production process concentrated on the transformation, storage, and transport of *material and energy;* in the post industrial era the accent is on transformation, storage, and transport of *information.* This shift is nowadays enhanced by the emergence of a new infrastructure: the computer networks. These networks, resulting from the 'marriage' between advanced information and communication technologies, form the basis for the accelerated informatization of society. A similar point is made by Arthur D. Little: 'Transition of the centre-of-gravity of economic activities from more traditional manufacturing-oriented industries and jobs to the newer information ones is characteristic of the immediately present years. (...) The informatization process propelled by powerful technological, economic and social forces is inevitable, accelerating, unrelenting, international, and total'.[5]

Like the decline of the industrial sector, the spectacular growth of the information sector supports the idea that we are entering a new historical period. Nevertheless, the significance of the statistical exercises à la Porat, which boil down to a redefinition of eco-

Table 2.2. Origin of the growth of the information sector in a number of Western countries.

	France		Sweden		United Kingdom		Germany	
	1954	1975	1960	1975	1951	1971	1950	1976
Agriculture	0.3	0.2	0.6	0.5	0.4	0.2	0.2	0.1
Industry	5.1	9.1	10.8	11.3	5.9	8.6	5.1	10.0
Services	14.9	22.8	14.6	23.1	20.4	26.8	13.0	22.7
Total information occupations	20.3	32.1	26.0	34.9	26.7	35.6	18.3	32.8

Source: See table 2.1.

nomic activities, must not be exaggerated. The question remains as to how much information technology is creating a trendshift in a more fundamental sense, and/or will do so in the future. In the following chapters we shall try to answer this question.

Theoretical frame of reference

Without further evidence we will assume that society changes during the course of time, in the sense that the past never repeats itself. We assume in other words that the Western world is involved in an *evolutionary* process. This process is often characterized by the stages of technological innovation as expressed by the division 'agricultural-industrial-information era'. Alongside technological innovation, however, society also evolves from a social point of view, as appears from the changing norms and values and the changing (basic) institutions such as family, work, church and state. In this book technological and social-cultural change play equally significant roles. The question of which takes precedence as the 'prime mover' behind the process of societal evolution is studiously avoided. (We do not wish to become embroiled in the centuries old philosophical debate concerning the primacy of materialistic versus idealistic explanations of history, or – more fundamentally – the primacy of physical as opposed to metaphysical explanations.) This does not deny that in certain periods technology may take the lead over social changes (denoted in the literature by the term 'cultural lag'), or that norms and institutions may stimulate or impede technological innovation.

In parts III and IV technology and the social environment will, for the sake of clarity, be analytically separated. In part V we will see how the two can be simultaneously utilized to preserve a competitive edge for Western economies now and in the future.

3. The industrial firm in historical perspective

Since the Industrial Revolution, the traditional craft type of production has gradually evolved into the industrial type with which we are familiar today. Analytically this transformation encompassed at least three distinct dimensions: the input of production (in particular: work), the organization of production and the output of production (the type of product). Taking a closer look at this transition will help us sharpen our view on the changes that are currently taking place.

Adam Smith

Perhaps the most striking observation of the industrialization process dates from 1776, the year in which the founder of economics, Adam Smith, published his 'Wealth of Nations'.[1] The core of the industrialization process lay, according to Smith, in the increasing *division of labour* which took on a specific form in his time. Of course, division of labour antedated the Industrial Revolution: early specialization gave rise to professions such as tailor, smith, carpenter, etc. During the Industrial Revolution, however, an extra dimension was added. Products were no longer produced by one man, or a few persons, but by a large number of employees performing mainly routine tasks. The term division of *work* is in fact better here than the more commonly used term division of *labour*. In this connection Bücher[2] (1893) made an illustrative distinction between the pre-industrial process of 'Berufsbildung' (the division of *labour,* from which the craft professions evolved) and the 'Arbeitserlegung' (the division of *work* during and after the Industrial Revolution).

The advantages of the division of work were evident: it resulted in a spectacular rise in productivity. Smith illustrates this by way of the famous example of a pin factory in Scotland. While one worker could only produce 20 pins per day at the most, in the small factory which Smith observed ten workers – of which one straightened the metal, another one cut it, yet another one sharpened the pins, etc. – could produce 4800 pins per day. The introduction of work division caused a multiplication of the production per worker from 20 to 480 pins.

At the same time, however, Smith also saw disadvantages. These mainly concerned the decrease in the quality of the work. The craft work-task was reduced to a monotonous repetition of simple tasks, resulting in a degradation of the requisite skill:

> The man whose whole life is spent in performing a few simple operations, of which the effects too are perhaps always the same, or very nearly the same, has no occasion to exert his understanding, or to exercise his invention . . . and generally becomes as stupid and ignorant as it is possible for a human creature to become.[3]

Taylor

The division of work which Smith observed expanded as technology advanced. A decisive push in this development was given around 1900 by Frederick W. Taylor – the founder of the 'Scientific Management School' – who, with his so-called 'time and motion studies', provided the reduction of complex operations into simple ones with a scientific base. Alongside horizontal division of work tasks, Taylor also pleaded for vertical differentiation between control and performance:

> All mental work should be exiled from the shop floor and should be centralized in planning and preparation departments so that the work of bosses, foremen, and workers is of an exclusively performance nature.[4]

The vertical differentiation Taylor pleaded for is in fact an inevitable extension of the horizontal differentiation already observed by Smith. Moreover, in Smith's pin factory, a separate management function evolved because the sharpening of 4800 pins per day, or in general, the performance of short cyclical repetitive work, is difficult to combine with simultaneous planning and control of the production process as a whole. In other words, *breaking up craft work into objective, depersonalized tasks inevitably makes it necessary to independently allocate the previously undifferentiated management function.* Employees and employers, and their related pressure groups evolved as inevitable by-products of the Industrial Revolution.

Wernet

A final aspect of the transformation of the craft work-place into the industrial factory is the altered function of capital goods. This change is not unrelated to the increasing differentiation of the production process, but illustrates it from another angle. In principle, capital goods can be utilized in two ways: (1) as a tool, as an

Table 3.1. The craft and industrial type of production characterized by way of input, organization and output.

	Craft	Industrial

Input	labour:
	– skilled
	– autonomous
	– creative
	capital:
	– tools,
	  capital goods as
	  extension to man
	  (personal technology)
		– simple
		– dependant
		– routine
		
		– machines, man as
		  extension to capital
		  goods (instrumental
		  technology)

Organization	– little or no work
	  division
	
	– little or no
	  seperation of
	  control-performance
	– small scale
		– extensive work division
		  (horizontal
		  differentiation)
		– formal seperation
		  control-performance
		  (vertical differentiation)
		– large scale

Output	– client orientated
	  products
		– mass products for
		  an anonymous market

extension to man; and (2) as a machine utilizing man as it's extension (an extreme example is the assembly line). In Wernet's 'Demarcation between craft and industry'[5] (1965) this dichotomy plays a central role. In the case of a craft type utilization of capital he speaks of a *personal work technique* in which the role of the machine is adapted to the worker. The reverse case, in which the machine fulfills a dominating role forcing the worker to adapt, defines an *instrumental work technique*. The characterization of the industrialization process by way of mutations which occur in the man-machine relationship dates from the end of the 18th century when Ferguson (1767) characterized the industrial work-place as 'an engine, the parts of which are men'.[6]

The various dimensions of the industrialization process which have been reviewed can be ordered as follows:
− With regard to the *input* in the production process, in particular *labour,* the share of skilled, autonomous work has declined. At the same time, capital has increasingly been transformed from creatively used tools into routinely operated machines.
− The *organizational structure* of firms has become ever more differentiated, both horizontally and vertically. Firms have grown larger and larger.
− With regard to *output,* customized products have increasingly been replaced by mass products for an anonymous market.

The historical trend from a craft-oriented economy to an indus-trialized economy can be summarized as a movement along a continuum with two opposing 'ideal types' at the endpoints, speci-fied in table 3.1. Generally speaking, this movement has been one from the left to the right, i.e. from the second to the third column of the table.

In Part III we shall consider − for each of the three dimensions (input, organization, output) − whether information technology is reinforcing or reversing the historical trend. When examining the consequences for work we shall consider both the quantity and the quality of work.

Part III: Information technology: a trendshift

The industrialization of the Western world since the end of the 18th century may be conceived as a process of continuous technological innovation. At present this innovation is based primarily on information technology. As in the past, the introduction of this technology is accompanied by capital intensification and productivity growth. Alongside however, information technology causes breaks with the past. As has already been mentioned, the share of industrial employment is declining, while at the same time the information sector has grown to become the largest sector. These sectoral shifts only give a limited view of the changes which are currently taking place. In this part we shall examine the changes in employment and in the quality of work (chapters 5 and 6), in the organization of firms (chapter 7), and in the type of product (chapter 8). At the same time, further consideration will be given to the nature of economic activities in the information sector (chapter 9).

4. Accelerating technological innovation

In the preceeding chapters the term 'technological innovation' has been loosely used without further specification or operationalization. What in fact is technological innovation? This question is answered differently depending on the disciplinary background, political conviction, and/or aim of the author.[1] A common denominator is lacking. Even over the classification of definitions there are differences of opinion. In this book, the term technological innovation is conceived as good old Schumpeter's[2] (1883–1950) 'neue Kombinationen': the innovation of the production process and of products. Not technological knowledge itself, i.e. the inventions, but the applications of this knowledge in the economy, i.e. the innovations, are our subject matter.

To operationalize technological innovation, various indicators can be considered, in particular:

I: the increase of productivity per worker, or per man hour;
II: the increase in capital intensity of the production process.

I. Econometricians have done a great deal of research on the contribution of technology to productivity growth. Estimates by Solow, Abramowitz, Denison (and others) vary, but all are high. A recent OECD report 'Microelectronics, productivity and employment'[3] states that approximately 80% of productivity growth (in the period 1950–1976) can be attributed to technological change. Including the increase in 'human capital', technology even explains a considerably higher percentage. Of course, technological innovation and productivity growth do not coincide; but in general they do keep in step. Time series of productivity growth therefore give a rough approximation of the rate of technological innovation.

II. Formally more exact is the use of capital intensity as an indicator. Innovation of the production process first of all takes place via investments in new capital goods. Product innovation (e.g. the application of integrated circuits in radios) is also accompanied by new investments: product innovation almost always implies process innovation. The increase in capital goods per worker can therefore be used as an indicator of the development of 'neue Kombinationen'. In the long run, capital intensification and productivity growth show (see below) a virtually parallel development.

To get a rough idea of the rate of technological innovation during the past 100 years, figure 4.1. shows the capital intensification for five countries in the period 1890–1980. By and large the same pattern prevails in every country: after a gradual increase from 1890 onwards, the post-war period (beginning about 1960) shows a historically unique acceleration. In the USA the difference in rate before and after the Second World War is least pronounced. The technological advantage over Europe has apparently become smaller in the post-war period. The diagram, by the way, gives little insight into absolute differences between individual countries. This is because capital intensity is measured in 1970 dollars (per man hour). Over or undervaluation of currencies may therefore distort the picture. The leading position taken by the Netherlands needs to be seen in this light.

The second indicator of technological innovation – productivity growth – shows a similar picture. Figure 4.2. exhibits the parallel course of the two indicators in the period 1963–1974 for eight Western countries. The indicators appear highly correlated: countries with high (low) productivity increase show a high (low) growth in capital intensity. The figure also confirms the acceleration of post war technological change in Europe compared to the USA noted earlier.

Table 4.1. gives an overview of the course of both indicators before and after the oil crisis in 1973. Most noticeable is that technological innovation – measured in terms of capital intensification – has continued at virtually the same high rate in the period 1973–1978 as in the period 1950–1973. Productivity growth did slow down, be it only temporarily. In the 1980s output per

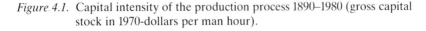

Figure 4.1. Capital intensity of the production process 1890–1980 (gross capital stock in 1970-dollars per man hour).

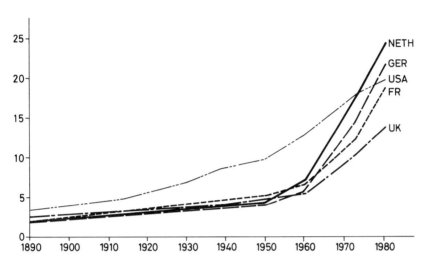

Source: Own calculation based on A. Maddison, *Phases of Capitalist Development*, Oxford University Press, 1982, tables III-5, C-5, C-9, D-8, D-9, D-12, and D-13.

manhour has improved sharply, particularly in the USA. Recent statistics from the US Department of Labor[4] show a 4.1% average annual increase in productivity in the manufacturing industries in the period 1981–1985, i.e. the highest increase by far since World

Table 4.1. Indicators of the rate of technological change before and after 1973 in six Western Countries.

	Growth of capital intensity[a]		Growth of labour productivity[b]	
	1950–1973	1973–1978	1950–1973	1973–1979
USA	2.9	1.8	2.6	1.4
Germany	6.1	6.3	6.0	4.2
France	4.5	5.3	5.1	3.5
Italy	5.4	6.3	5.8	2.5
UK	4.0	4.3	3.1	2.1
The Netherlands	6.3	5.3	4.4	3.1

a. Fixed capital stock.
b. Gross domestic product per man hour.

Source: A. Maddison, *Phases of Capitalist Development*, Oxford University Press, 1982.

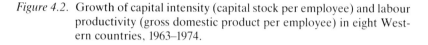

Figure 4.2. Growth of capital intensity (capital stock per employee) and labour productivity (gross domestic product per employee) in eight Western countries, 1963–1974.

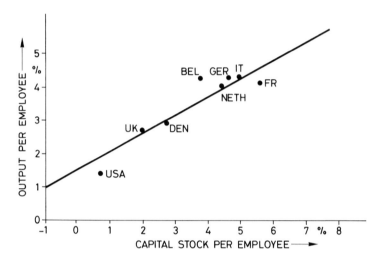

Source: John P. Stein and Allen Lee, *Productivity growth in industrial countries at the sectoral level 1963–1974*, The Rand Corporation, 1977, table S.1.

War II. Manufacturing output, as measured by the Federal Reserve Board's index, has increased nearly 30% since 1982! Information technology appears to have taken over from other innovations as the principal source of productivity growth.[5]

To summarize, the following broad conclusions may be drawn:
– technological innovation in the last 100 years shows a considerable acceleration from the 1960s onwards (more pronounced in Europe than in the USA, the leading industrial country);
– the high post-war rate seems to have decreased only slightly after the oil crisis in 1973;
– in the 1980s information technology has pushed the rate of innovation/productivity growth in the US manufacturing industries to a level higher than ever before.

5. Reduced working hours

Without falling into a deterministic trap, it can be stated that during the last 100 years technological innovation has drastically changed society. With regard to work, there has been a change both in a quantitative and a qualitative sense. In this chapter we will limit ourselves to the quantitative aspect. As will become apparent, the relative significance of work continually declined in the past. Capital intensification meant replacement of human work by machines. Until recently this replacement – apart from the compensating effects of economic growth – has gradually been taken up by a reduction in working hours. By and large demand and supply on the labour market remained in balance. However, information technology may very well change this scene.

Working hours in historical perspective

A declining significance of labour compared to capital was predicted by various 'classical' economists, particularly by Marx. After Marx the interest in this topic has been fairly small. Recently however, with the introduction of information technology and the increased unemployment in all Western countries, the discussions about technology as a 'job killer' and 'jobless growth' have flared up again. Few realize, however, that the relative significance of work has declined continually during the industrial age. True enough not so much in the form of direct labour displacement, but rather by a reduction in the number of working hours. Generation after generation, working hours per year have declined, while the standard of living nevertheless rose spectacularly as a result of the same technological progress.

Figure 5.1. shows the decline in the number of working hours

Figure 5.1. Working hours[a] per employee per year for four countries, 1890–1980.

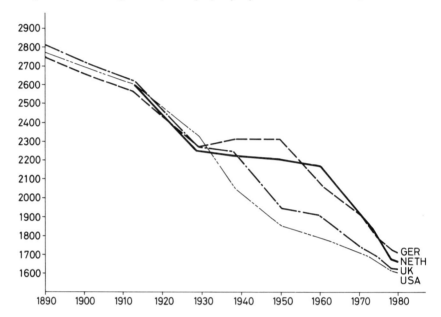

a. 'Working hours' equal the contracted working hours corrected for vacations, public
   holidays, and sick leave.

Source: A. Maddison, *Phases of Capitalist Development,* Oxford University Press, 1982,
   table C-9.

per year for four industrialized countries during the period 1890–
1980. Although the statistical material for the first decades (1890–
1929) is based on fairly rough estimates, the total view is un-
mistakeable: in all countries the number of working hours has
been almost halved during the last 100 years. This reduction seems
to be taking place like an evolutionary trend.

Capital intensification and reduction in working hours

The relationship between capital intensification and reduction in
working hours in seven Western countries is reproduced for the
statistically most reliable period, 1960–1980, in table 5.1. and
figure 5.2. The table gives two measurements of both variables.
The increase in capital intensity between 1960–1980 is expressed
as an index number (column 1), and as an average percentage

Table 5.1. Capital intensification and reduction in working hours in the period
1960–1980 in a number of Western countries.

	Capital intensification of the production process 1960–1980		Reduction in working hours[a] 1960–1980	
	(1) 1980 (1960 = 100)	(2) perc. change (av. p.a.)	(3) no. of hours	(4) perc. change (av. p.a.)
The Netherlands	280,07	5,28	521	1,36
Germany	297,51	5,60	381	1,00
France	239,50	4,46	268	0.72
Italy[b]	261,77	5,49	493	1,51
UK	204,08	3,63	310	0,88
USA	138,40	1,64	197	0,58
Canada[c]	145,60	2,00	147	0,43

a. see figure 5.1.
b. 1960–1978.
c. 1960–1979.

Source: Own calculation based on A. Maddison, *Phases of Capitalist Development,*
Oxford University Press, 1982. Eurostat, *National Accounts Statistics, 1982.*

Figure 5.2. Capital intensification ($\Delta K/L$) and reduction of working hours (ΔT_l)
in seven Western countries, 1960–1980 (column (1) and (3) from
table 5.1.).

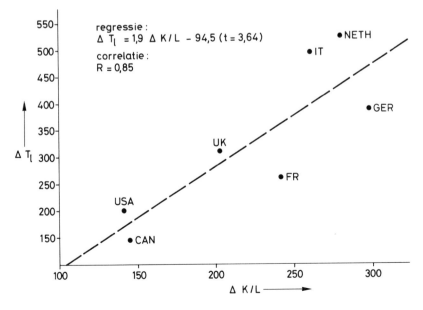

increase (column 2); the reduction in working hours as the number of hours (column 3), and a percentage decline (column 4).
Figure 5.2. shows the correlation between column (1) and (3) (the
relationship between (2) and (4) has not been reproduced, but is
almost identical). Generally speaking, the diagram shows a significant relationship between the rate of technological change and
reduction in working hours: countries with a relatively rapidly
increasing capital intensity, such as the Netherlands, Germany,
and Italy also show a more rapid decline in working hours; on the
other hand, in countries with a relatively slow increase in capital
intensity, such as the USA and Canada, the number of working
hours declines relatively slowly. Finally, two countries, England
and France, take up a position more or less in between. The
calculated correlation coefficient between both variables
amounts to 0.85 (t = 3.64), which explains a considerable part of
the variance.

Figure 5.3. – from Zegveld and Rothwell[1] – illustrates for virtually
the same period (1958–1980), the relationship between technological change and the quantity of work in the industrial sector
in the USA and nine EEC countries. The diagram – constructed
for another purpose, but serving ours just as well – measures
industrial production on the x-axis, and industrial employment on
the y-axis. During the period 1958–1980, industrial production in
the USA, and the EEC appears to have risen at virtually the same
rate. On the other hand, industrial employment has increased
strongly in the USA, but declined in the EEC. This divergence
can be explained by the rate of technological innovation which has
risen more strongly in the EEC than in the USA. Accelerated
innovation in Europe has not led to more, but to less employment, which occurred together with a relatively faster rise in per
capita income.

From the correlation between technological innovation and declining working hours in figure 5.2. the following future scenario
can be deduced. Assuming that the *rate* of innovation (of capital
intensification) in 1980–2000 will be similar to the average in the
period 1960–1980 of the countries listed in table 5.1. (considering
the potential contribution of information technology, the future

Figure 5.3. The development of industrial employment and production in the
USA and EEC-9 in the period 1958–1980.

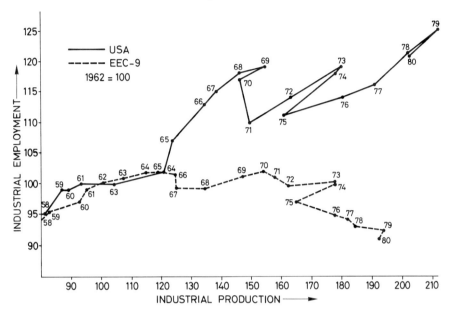

Source: R. Rothwell and W. Zegveld, *Innovations and the Small and Medium Sized Firms*, Frances Pinter (Publishers) London, 1982, p. 254.

innovation rate may even be higher), it can be calculated that by
the year 2000 working hours should have declined by an additional 25% in order to prevent rising unemployment. How such
a reduction is to be accomplished, through stimulating part-time
work, early retirement or otherwise, remains to be seen.

Conclusion

1. Contrary to what is often assumed, accelerated technological
    innovation decreases rather than increases employment (as-
    suming this acceleration takes place simultaneously in all
    countries). The faster the introduction of new technologies,
    the more urgent the need for a reduction in working hours.
    (To prevent misunderstanding: technology is not the only
    determinant of the number of working hours. The rate of
    economic growth, demographic factors, etc. also play a role.

In the long run, however, technological innovation does seem
to have the most significant impact.)

2. Information technology is likely to create more unemployment unless we parallel the innovation based on this technology with a drastic reduction of the (average) number of working hours.

6. Higher quality work

The industrialization of Western economies brought about a decline in the quality of work. Industrialization stands for degradation and deskilling; craft work has increasingly been replaced by routine factory work. The question is whether or not information technology will reinforce or reverse this trend. A first indication may be derived from the collective decline of the industrial sector in Western countries. True enough this decline does not automatically imply an average upgrading, but one might expect to see a global effect. Work division is most advanced in the industrial sector: an increase (decrease) in the economic significance of this sector can therefore be regarded as a decrease(increase) of the quality of work as a whole. In the words of John Evans[1]:

> Surveys that have been carried out to assess the factors that are conducive to the application of microelectronics have shown that it is particularly suitable in automating industrial processes where existing jobs involve tasks which are repetitive or sequentially repetitive. Much of the development of industrialised societies has involved the creation of such jobs, through the division of labour, specialization of tasks and mechanization of production processes.

More specifically, the change in the quality of work can be measured by what is known in the literature as the *work content*. This term covers both the requisite skill-level and the related degree of work autonomy. From a historical perspective, the change in the work content is usually divided into three stages.[2]

In the first, pre-industrial stage, production is primarily based on hand work, characterized by a relatively high skill-level. Technology serves simply as a tool, i.e. as an extension of man.

The second industrial stage is characterized by the introduction of machines, i.e. by mechanization. The nature, methods, and rate of work become dependant on the pace of the machine. This development is accompanied by a degradation of the work content. Statistical evidence to support this decline is scarce. The only source that we could find is the doctoral thesis by Van der Waerden[3] in 1911 entitled 'Education level and technology'. On the basis of two business censuses in Germany in the years 1895 and 1907, the author notes 'a decline in the number of skilled workers'. This decline includes all sectors apart from the so called 'artistic crafts'. The 'paper industry' and the 'leather industry' score very high with a decline of 14%. There is also a substantial decline in the 'metal processing', 'chemical industry', 'textile industry', 'wood processing', and 'sanitation sector', varying from 7 to 10%. For all sectors together, the proportion of skilled workers declined in the period 1895–1907 by 7.1% (from 64.8% to 57.7%).

In the third and last stage starting in the 1950s, work is gradually taken over by autonomous technical systems, i.e. by automation. As far as the impact on work is concerned, the literature is divided into two camps. On the one hand, it is expected that the negative aspects of industrial work will gradually disappear. Touraine[4] for example, thinks that work will gain in content and autonomy, and will require new and higher-level skills. This is also recognized by Blauner[5] who thinks that automation will put an end to the situation of dependance and alienation characteristic of the preceeding stage. He is also optimistic about the impact of automation on the skill-level. Contrary to this optimism however, is the sombre vision of authors such as Braverman[6], and (until recently) Kern and Schumann.[7] According to them there is nothing new; automation continues the 'deskilling' trend of the industrial age. Only the work of the highest personnel is not affected, and in a number of cases even improves. However, a vast majority is 'downgraded' which leads to increasing polarization.

The question whether or not the historical trend towards degradation is reversed is therefore answered differently. The number of affirmative answers is nevertheless increasing. The most convincing is perhaps the recent about-face of Kern and Schumann, two of the most authoritative supporters of the degradation/ polarization thesis. In their last publications[8] the authors literally note 'a trendbreak in the way labour is utilized in the production process'. If entrepreneurs in the past 'only made a minimum use of the potential contribution of labour', at the moment the authors see a trend in the direction of 'a more complete utilization of the worker's potential'. This trendbreak can, according to the authors, be explained by both technological and social changes. The last category includes for example the noticeable change in management attitudes. Instead of regarding workers as 'warm bodies' who 'function most efficiently when they are put to work under the most accurate and restrictively formulated rules, and under the sharpest and most extensive regime of control (. . .), nowadays a worker is regarded, at least by the more enlightened managers as a person with complex talents and a vast potential'. According to the authors, information technology, contrary to technology in the past, creates the possibility of 'a reintegration of work tasks', and of 'a reintroduction of skilled workers' and 'professionalization of work'. Their evidence is particularly based on observations in the automobile, the machine and the chemical industry.

More generally, recent literature increasingly emphasizes the opportunities offered by information technology for the reintegration and upgrading of work. What is more, there is evidence that these opportunities have to be utilized as otherwise firms tend to lose their competitive edge.[9] In the UK Enid Mumford (Manchester Business School)[10] has shown that office automation can simultaneously improve the quality of work and increase profits. In the USA the discussion on this point has particularly been stimulated by Robert Reich[11] who sees reintegration as a precondition for the maintenance of America's competitive edge. In a provocative manner he outlines the bankruptcy of 'standardized, high volume production' which should be replaced by 'highly integrated systems of production based on merger of traditionally separate business functions (design, engineering, purchasing, manufacturing, distribution, marketing, sales) that can respond quickly to new market opportunities (. . .) The distinction heretofore drawn between those who plan work and those who execute work is inappropriate'. Information technology therefore holds the promise of easing and even abolishing a traditional conflict of the industrial age between workers and employers. Reintegration and broadened autonomy, or to put it differently, the return to craft-type work, not only benefit the worker but also the company results.

Without a doubt, however, the potential contribution of information technology to the quality of work has not yet materialized. This is not surprising; conventional wisdom often prevails. Among managers the idea that upgrading and profits are not incompatable is only slowly gaining ground. Nevertheless, there are some encouraging developments. For example, Spenner (1979)[12] concludes (by comparing the data contained in two sequential editions of the 'Dictionary of Occupational Titles'), that 'there has been a slight upgrading in skill requirements in several sectors of the labor force in the last 10–12 years'. Rumberger (1981)[13] also notes 'that between 1960 and 1976 changes in the distribution of employment have favored skilled jobs, while changes in the skill requirements of individual occupations have tended to narrow the distribution of job skills. Overall the average skill requirements increased in this period'. Conen and Huygen[14] in the Netherlands have made comparable observations on changes in quality of work in the period 1960–1977. Their conclusion, based on samples from the 1960, 1971 and 1977 Censuses, is that in the period 1960–1977 there was a slight upgrading of the quality of work. This upgrading took place despite a degradation in some sectors. This paradoxical fact can, according to the authors, be explained by the 'rapidly growing category of higher employees within the total working population'. Along the lines of Rumberger's conclusion, it appears that the overall upgrading of work is caused by shifts between categories.

Finally, one may point to research results in which work content (skill level and autonomy), appears to vary inversely with the size of the firm (measured by the number of employees).[15] Anticipating chapter 7, in which it will appear that the average size of firms has declined since 1970, these results support the assumption that the quality of work has recently improved.

Summarizing, we note that although time series which accurately measure the quality of work are not available, there is nevertheless good reason to assume a trendshift in the continuing degradation of work during the industrial past. The evidence to support

this trendshift has recently increased. This is also apparent for the
man-machine relationship which we will now examine.

The development of the man-machine relationship: a trendshift?

In 1958 Peter Drucker[16] wrote: 'What is called automation today is
a conceptual and logical extension of Taylor's Scientific Management'. In other words, automation meant a continuation of the
historical process of work division, of replacing 'tools' by machines. However, after the 1950s the dominant type of automation
changed. If at first one could only speak of *rigid* automation,
exclusively applicable in mass production, nowadays a new trend
can be seen – *flexible* production automation (fpa) – with poten-
tially radical consequences for the man-machine relationship.
Flexible automation means that a large number of different products can be manufactured by one programmable apparatus. With
regard to the man-machine relationship, flexible production automation in fact offers a choice between enhanced Taylorization
and a more tool-like use of capital goods. This choice is clearly
described in a recent report from the 'Netherlands Study Centre
for Technology Trends'[17]:

> With flexible automation we can follow a different path to
> that of 'scientific management'. A choice has to be made
> between capital goods which enforce programmed behaviour
> (machines), and those which extend human skills (tools).
> This choice is not only limited to the shopfloor, but is also
> relevant for all other functions. Technically the potential for
> developing new tools is available . . .

The dilemma is similar to an earlier one discussed by Noble.[18] In
the early 1950s, a choice had to be made between 'numerical
control' (NC), a Tayloristic application of automation, and 'record playback', in which a continuous call had to be made on the
worker's skills. With 'record playback' a machine operator makes
a part, and his movements are simultaneously recorded on a
magnetic tape. After the operation is completed, identical parts
can be manufactured by 'playing back the tape' which then re-

produces the recorded movements. Numerical control involves a
totally different approach. A mathematical representation of a
part must be found which facilitates a description of the requisite
tool-movements that can be broken down into hundreds or thou-
sands of separate instructions which can be translated into a
compact numerical code and read by a control unit. The NC-tape
makes the worker's skill superfluous. Around 1950 the NC-system
was preferred. In the more advanced NC machines of today
similar choices are being made. That the results can widely differ
is illustrated in the following description of an American and a
Norwegian application of NC-machines[19]:

First the description of the US plant:
> Machine operators are not permitted to edit programs –
> much less to make their own – on the new CNC (Computer
> Numerical Control) machines; quite often the controls are
> locked. Only supervisory staff and programmers are allowed
> to edit the programs. (. . .) The shortcomings of this system
> for the operators are obvious. Less obvious are the shortcom-
> ings for management: lower quality production and excessive
> machine down time. If the programs are faulty and the opera-
> tor cannot (or is not allowed to) make necessary adjustment
> the parts produced will be faulty (. . .), with a corresponding
> loss of productivity.

Next, the Norwegian plant:
> (. . .) the operators routinely do all the editing, according to
> their own criteria of safety, efficiency, quality, and con-
> venience: they change the sequence of operations, add or
> subtract operations, and sometimes alter the entire structure
> of the program to suit themselves. (. . .) All operators are
> trained in NC programming and, as a consequence, their
> conflicts with the programmers are reduced. One program-
> mer (. . .) justified having any programmers at all by the fact
> that the programmer was a specialist and was thus more
> proficient.

Conclusion

1. In the industrial age the relative significance of highly qualified and autonomous work has declined. For at least two
   reasons the information age will show (is showing) a reversal
   of this trend. First of all, computers and robots displace un-
   skilled routine work much more frequently than highly qualified complex tasks. If one imagines a continuum with, on the
   left, the latter category, and, on the right, the first category,
   then information technology engulfs, so to speak, the continuum from right to left.

2. The second reason is more complicated and involves a crucial
   choice on the part of management. Information technology
   can be applied both to decrease and to increase the quality of
   work, to narrow and to broader the degree of autonomy, and
   to degrade and upgrade work. The latter application not only
   benefits the worker, but also strengthens the firm's competitive edge.

3. Information technology can be applied both as a tool (as an
   extension of human skill) and as a machine (forcing the
   worker to keep its pace). A choice for the first type of application has consequences similar to those described under the
   heading of work upgrading in 2.

7. The decline of the large-scale factory

In this chapter we shall examine the organizational changes brought about by the introduction of information technology. The central question will be whether not only the degradation of work, but also the simultaneous rise of the large-scale factory has reached its peak. We will first focus on the interaction between technological innovation and organizational change in the past, and will then go on to examine how this interaction will develop in the future.

Organization theory has divergent traditions and the position we take must first be clarified. Explanations of long-run organizational change fall into two types. According to the first, technology is seen as the 'prime mover', to which social reality – including the organizational structure of firms – adapts. Classic representatives of this line of thought are, for example, Mumford[1] and Veblen.[2] Among modern authors, Galbraith[3] and Toffler[4] should be mentioned. The second type conceives technology as an integral part of social reality. Technologically induced changes, in which technology is regarded exogenously, are excluded. This type can be subdivided into voluntarists and determinists. According to the voluntarists, the organizational structure primarily reflects the will of a power elite. Braverman,[5] and Kern and Schumann[6] represent this line of thought. Determinists, on the other hand, emphasize the impact of social-cultural factors which cannot, or hardly ever, be influenced. An important example of such a factor is the increasing rationalization of (Western) culture. In this connection one of the founders of sociology should be mentioned – Max Weber[7] – who regarded the increasing rationalization/bureaucratization of firms as a part of the rationalizing trend in society as a whole.

In this book, as explained in chapter 2, we regard technology and social reality as interdependant phenomena. Without committing ourselves to either one of the two types, we will treat these phenomena – for the sake of clarity – as analytically separate. In this part we will confine ourselves to the impact of technology. Thus, we will defer treatment of the rise, spread, and decline of Taylorism until part IV.

The size of the firm in historical perspective

At the time of the Industrial Revolution the organizational structure of firms (principally craft work places) was characterized by a low degree of differentiation, both in a horizontal and vertical sense. On the vertical dimension, control and performance of work were highly integrated; hierarchy did exist, but the number of layers was extremely limited. Work was also horizontally integrated, division of work among workers and/or departments hardly ever occurred. Related to this, the number of workers per firm was small. A precise answer as to whether or not the connection between the degree of work division and the size of the firm is concave, convex or a straight line is hard to give (see figure 7.1.). What is certain however is that organizational differentiation is linked to increasing size.[8]

To gain some insight into the degree of differentiation of firms in the long run, we shall use the size of the firm as an indicator. Although time series of the average size (per geographical establishment, not per firm as a judicial unit) are not available, we can nevertheless construct a general view of the last 50 years. Before going on to this, however, we shall take a brief look at the literature.

According to De Jonge,[9] in his study 'The industrialization of The Netherlands, 1850–1914', the core of the industrialization process lay in the rise of factory-type production. In this period the production process in the West went through what he calls 'the classic structure change': an increase in the size of production units. This process of increasing scale is indicative of the declining significance of the craft sector. Division of work, increasing scale, and the rise of the industrial sector developed in parallel. Never-

Figure 7.1. Possible correlations between the division of work and the size of the firm.

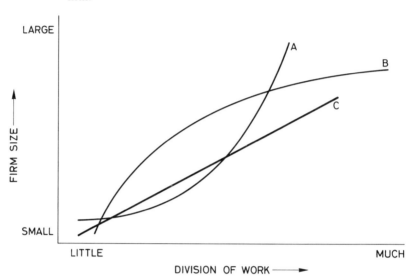

theless, as Lewis Mumford emphasizes in his classic 'Technics and Civilization' (1934), the factory as an organization type existed before the Industrial Revolution in an elementary form. With water and wind as power sources, factory settings were experimented with before the arrival of the steam engine. The discontinuity caused by the steam engine can be interpreted as the acceleration of a nascent development.

Gradually, technology fueled the transformation of the craft work-place into the factory by means of a large number of inventions and innovations. They can be summarized in the following categories:
– *power sources* (steam engine, electricity);
– *transportation* (railways, automobiles, aeroplanes);
– *communication* (telegraph, telephone);
– *information processing* (digital computer, microprocessor).

The period 1750–1900 may be characterized as the 'steam-railway-telegraph era'. The steam engine made it possible to concentrate machines and workers under one roof. Railways promoted transport of raw materials over long distances, and the distribution of end products over widespread markets. The telegraph, linked to the railways, further strengthened the concentration.

Fundamental improvements in power, transport, and communications occurred in the period 1900–1950, which can be characterized as the 'electricity-automobile-telephone era'. However, the innovations based on these inventions reached their peak during the last decades. By and large technological innovation and the growing size of firms were strongly intertwined, as, among others, Galbraith emphasized in his 'New Industrial State' (1967).

The most revolutionary element of technological change during the last decades was undoubtedly the discovery of the electronic digital computer. Due to this invention the rate of innovation has reached a historically unprecedented level. Before examining the influence of information technology on the size of the firm, we shall take a look at the statistics.

Figure 7.2. shows the average firm size in the industrial sector for four countries from 1930 onwards. Statistical evidence for other sectors and before 1930 is not available. The calculations for the Netherlands and Germany include the self-employed. For England and the USA, this category does not date back far enough. Despite the heterogeneity of the statistical sources, the graphs give a fairly reliable view of the long-run development in the average firm size (the calculation is specified in the Appendix). Generally speaking, the trend is the same for all countries. From 1930 up until around 1970 there was a marked increase. Although statistics earlier than 1930 are not available, this increase may be regarded as a continuation of an earlier trend. Around 1970 this trend reached a peak, after which – most probably for the first time in history – a simultaneous decline has taken place in all countries. The trendshift more or less coincides with the reversal in the degradation of work noted earlier.

The trendshift appears to be the result of multiple causes. Undoubtedly it is related to the recession, as a consequence of which many companies have been forced to cut down on personnel. Moreover, the recession, just as in the 1930s, has led to the rise of many (one-man) small firms which decreases the average firm

Figure 7.2. The average size of the firm in the industrial sector in historical perspective (The Netherlands and Germany: persons per establishment; USA and UK: employees per establishment).

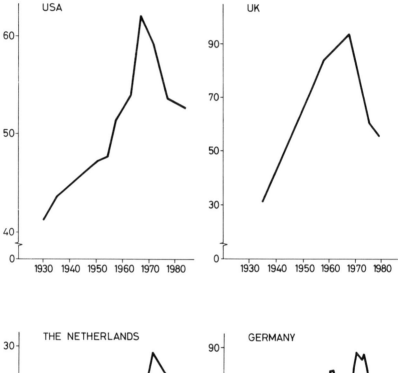

Source and remarks: See Appendix.

size. At the same time, however, information technology has contributed to the trendshift in various ways.

The impact of information technology on the size of some multinationals has already been mentioned (see figure 2.2.). In these multinationals, employment reached a peak around 1970, and then started to decline. The introduction of information technology and a declining size appeared to be two sides of the same coin. The end of this development, as foreseen by the OECD in 1981, is coming into view: 'the completely automated factory: small cells of numerically controlled machine tools, fed by robots, controlled by minicomputers and linked in turn to a central computer regulating the flow of work and materials'.[10]

A second cause of the trendshift lies in the previously unknown high rate of (information) technological change and the accompanying turbulence in the market. A large-scale, differentiated organization functions excellently as long as technology advances relatively slowly and markets are relatively stable. Until the 1960s these conditions were more or less fulfilled. Since then the market has become ever more turbulent. An adequate response to the turbulence inside and outside the firm presupposes much more flexibility than the old style mammoths can muster. To meet the challenge of the information age little less than a revolution is needed. The main elements of this revolution are debureaucratization, decentralization, reintegration of functions and reduction in scale. In short, a reverse of the differentiation process characteristic of the industrial past. It is this type of about-face which Reich[11] advocates in his 'Next American Frontier' when he pleads for the introduction of 'flexible production systems'.

The attractive part of information technology is – and this is the most crucial point – that this technology can be implemented so as to facilitate the kind of debureaucratization and reintegration that modern firms must embrace to survive. In chapter 20 some leading edge pioneers will be discussed. In general, the reversal of the historical trends has particularly been triggered by three major break-throughs:

– The micro-mainframe link, which facilitates on-line interaction with the mainframe from anywhere in the organization. With on-line, interactive systems the formerly segmented tasks have

been given back to the individuals and work groups who then
have greater autonomy, easier access to computerized records
(and part centres), and once again an integrated flow to their
work. For managers and staff professionals, the move to
on-line, interactive systems and database systems increases the
ease with which they can access data for information retrieval
and analysis;
- Advanced, user-friendly (fourth generation) software, which
  allows non-experts to perform complicated operations;
- Computernetworks, which link users throughout an organization and make rigid, hierarchical patterns of information flow
  obsolete.

In this connection, the Dutch author De Sitter[12] also deserves to
be mentioned. In his book 'Towards new factories and offices' (in
Dutch) he shows by way of 20 case studies that the application of
information technology has indeed led to both a less differentiated production organization and, at the same time, to more
efficiency. His book is in fact a plea for a break with past conventional wisdom in order to meet the present challenge.
    Finally, we shall mention Toffler[13] who also bases the need for
firms to transform into more flexible, small-scale organizations on
the historically unprecedented acceleration of technological
change:

> Each age produces a form of organization appropriate to its
> own tempo. During the long epoch of agricultural civiliza-
> tion, societies were marked by low transcience ... Organiza-
> tions were seldom called upon to make what we would regard
> as high-speed decisions. The age of industrialism brought a
> quickened tempo to both industrial and organizational life.
> Indeed, it was precisely for this reason that bureaucratic
> forms were needed ... With all rules codified, with a set of
> fixed principles indicating how to deal with various work
> problems, the flow of decisions could be accelerated to keep
> up with the faster pace of life brought by industrialism ... In
> the post-industrial society the acceleration of change has
> reached so rapid a pace that even bureaucracy can no longer
> keep up. Information surges through society so rapidly, dras-
> tic changes in technology come so quickly that newer, even

more instantly responsive forms of organization must characterize the future ... People in these organizations will be
differentiated not vertically, according to rank and role, but
flexible and functionally, according to skill and professional
training ... Skill will become more important, due to the
growing needs for collaboration in complex tasks.

Conclusion

1. In the industrial age technological innovation was accom-
    panied by a continuing expansion of (the average size of) firms
    and a continuing bureaucratization/differentiation of their or-
    ganizational structure.

2. Information technology offers unique opportunities for re-
    versing this trend. First of all, 'large' tends to become 'smaller'
    because of the displacement of the disproportionate amount
    of routine work in large firms. Secondly, the micro-mainframe
    link, advanced software and computer networks offer the
    opportunity for reversing the historical trend towards bu-
    reaucratization/differentiation of firms.

3. Due to the acceleration of change in the firm's environment
    the economies of scale (and of bureaucratization) have now
    turned into diseconomies. Managers are therefore forced to
    stimulate the reversal by simultaneously innovating their firms
    both technologically *and socially*. The penalty for clinging to
    conventional wisdom is a erosion of the competitive edge.

8. Individualized goods and services

In the industrial age, tailor made (craft) products have lost ground to (industrial) mass products. In this chapter we shall examine the role of information technology in reversing this trend.

To each mode of production since the Industrial Revolution one can associate distinctive product-types. Three such modes of production may be identified:
- mechanization (1800–1950);
- automation (1950–1970);
- flexible automation, computer networks: the 'informatization' of the production process (1970–present).

The impact of mechanization on the output of the economy can be summarized by two terms: greater uniformity and volume increase. With the increase in differentiation of organizations, and the increasing standardization and interchangeability of parts, efficiency and economies of scale rose dramatically. Although the standard of living increased, the range of choice per product decreased. Illustrative of this is Henry Ford's remark: 'You can have a car in any color as long as it's black'. Mass products, not designed to suit individual taste, flooded the market.

Automation got under way before 1950, but it was not until the 1950s, with the introduction of first generation digital computers, that it took off on a larger scale. Two types of automation prevailed in this period: process control and transfer automation (automation in which activities were carried out according to a fixed program). Process control was applied in industries such as chemicals, steel and oil refining. Transfer automation was applied in discrete-part production, mainly in the automobile industry. To be sure, both types of automation were justified on the grounds of increasing efficiency and economies of scale. However, another innovation in this period – numerical control used in aircraft manufacturing – meant a first step on the way towards flexible automation.

The third and most recent phase first took off thanks to the development of the relatively inexpensive and reliable micro-processor. As a basis for computers and control systems, micro-processors made it possible to transform factories and offices into flexible and adaptive production organizations. For both material and information products, the new technology stimulated a pro-duction system which promotes quality, diversity and individu-ality. More specifically, in industry we are dealing with computer integrated manufacturing (CAD/CAM) and in 'office automa-tion' with computer networks.

Computer integrated manufacturing provides the basis for the renewed rise of individualized products. 'Integrated' refers to the linking of different phases of the production process, in particular design and manufacturing. Products, or parts, are designed, mod-ified and perfected with the help of a computer-based graphics system (CAD). The manufacturing side, (CAM), refers to all the operations necessary after the design phase. CAD and CAM are integrated if they both make use of the same database and have access to the same product specifications. The designs which have been developed with the help of a graphics system, and which are stored in the computer, can also be used by the manufacturing division. The time and costs which are necessary to translate a design into the operations needed to produce a product are dras-tically reduced by this process. Furthermore, it is possible to reintroduce the customer/client into the design process. Designs can be quickly and easily modified to suit customer preference, and translated into manufacturing operations. Linked to flexible, computer controlled machines, and/or tools which can easily be programmed for the production of different parts, a revival of customized products is achieved. As Dertouzos[1] puts it: 'The biggest benefit of computerized automation lies in the tailoring of products and services to the most variable of demand centers – ourselves'.

Apart from the output of the industrial sector, information technology also influences the output of services. Computer networks in fact have the same significance for services as do CAD and CAM for material goods. By providing different forms of communication – computer to computer, computer to man, man to computer, and man to man – combined with a large variety of software and databases, computer networks can also serve as a medium for more individualized services. They facilitate interactions between people who cannot be in the same place at the same time. The databases available through the network serve as a shared memory, and the network's software extends the worker's scope and productivity. In the insurance industry, for example, it is now possible for one worker to deal with all the separate tasks required to complete and handle a contract, tasks which used to be spread over a number of different workers. The client is dealing with only one person in the company, offering him services tailored to his individual requirements (see also the case studies in chapter 20).

The application of information technology in the economy once again appears to support a trendshift. Contrary to the trend in the industrial past, the market orientation of firms is changing from mass products to more custom tailored goods and services. Statistical evidence to support this reorientation is as yet scarce. Time series of the *average batch size* – a possible indicator of the individualization of final products – are hardly ever kept by firms. Figure 8.1. shows – as an exception – the systematic decline of the average batch size of a product in the electronic sector in the 1970s. The figure is illustrative of the transformation which managers report anecdotally in all kinds of industries.

The fine-tuning of goods and services to individual requirements is very likely to develop further in the future. The arrival of the fifth generation computer (artificial intelligence) will simplify the development of software and make computers more accessible. This will further broaden the areas in which flexible automation and networks can be applied.

Finally, a marginal note. Modern information technology has made it possible to make individual products in a typical factory setting. For example, in the bicycle industry, a robot connected to a 12-armed welding machine with 24 degrees of freedom can, with

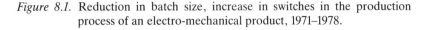

Figure 8.1. Reduction in batch size, increase in switches in the production
            process of an electro-mechanical product, 1971–1978.

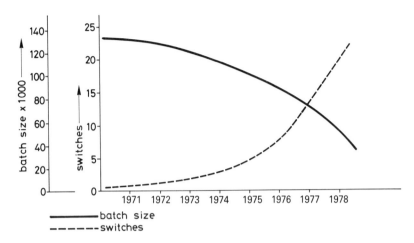

Source: H.J. Warnecke and B.H. Zippe, Arbeits- und Ablaufgestaltung in der Fertigung,
        in: *Zeitschrift für industrielle Fertigung 70* (1980), pp. 191–204.

a simple press of a button, quickly and without any difficulty,
change from one type of bicycle frame to another. Individual
frames can be produced separately and purely on order without
any special skills required. In these cases the next step will be the
completely automated, unmanned factory.

Conclusion

During the industrial age, custom tailored production was replaced at an increasing rate by mass produced goods manufactured for an anonymous market. Due to the impact of information
technology, this historical trend is nowadays being reversed. This
trendshift on the supply side of the market is complemented and
reinforced by changes in consumer preference, as will be set out
more fully in chapter 14.

9. New firms in the information sector

Thus far we have examined the impact of information technology in the context of the traditional three sectors: agriculture, industry, services. Information technology justifies – as we saw in chapter 2 – adding a fourth sector, in which all information activities are combined: the information sector. Not only does the information sector generate new employment, it also contributes to the trendshifts which have been examined in the previous chapters. As Lamborghini suggests: '(it is) mainly the work of craftsmen, essentially based on the individual skills of analysts and programmers'.[1] Like traditional craftsmen, the information worker requires a high level of skill, although the accent has changed from 'handcrafts' to 'mindcrafts'. Moreover, work in this sector is characterized by a high degree of autonomy, in which creativity is a major determinant of success. Microcomputers and processors are the new 'tools' which are applied within the new infrastructure (computer networks). The organization of firms in the information sector is relatively undifferentiated. Furthermore, the goods and services rendered meet a specific demand.

The following examples of firms in the information sector (summarized in table 9.1.) are all characterized by skilled and creative work, by a simple organization structure and by the aim of meeting a specific demand. They can be differentiated according to specific applications of information technology:
1. microcomputers;
2. computer networks;
3. microprocessors.

1. Activities based on *microcomputers* can be divided into:
    a. software development;

Table 9.1. New economic activities in the information sector.

Microcomputers

  Software development

  general applications
    accountancy programs for small firms
    job costing programs
    database management programs
    appointment scheduling programs
    business graphics packages
    stock control

  sector specific applications
    software for health care, education, industrial design
    production planning programs
    traffic control programs

  Specialized services

    computer employment agencies
    system development bureaus
    business and legal advice bureaus
    automation consultancy bureaus
    training institutes
    computer rental
    'manual service' bureaus
    computer camps

  Marketing

    computer fairs
    distribution of software packages
    publication of software packages

Networks

    on line information products
      electronic publications and news services
      databank communication (Teletext)
      on line education and training
      computer and tele-conferencing

Microprocessors

    security (home and business)
    energy consumption monitoring
    control systems (quality and production progress control)

b. specialized services;
c. marketing.

a. Software development involves writing programs designed to be run on microcomputers. Two subcategories can be distinguished: general applications and sector specific applications. General applications include a variety of programs for businesses and professional offices. Those which are used most are programs to handle financial transactions and databases for mailing lists. Sector specific applications include made-to-measure packages for doctors and engineers ('expert-programs') and administrative programs. Educational software is primarily used for learning with the aid of microcomputers.

b. Specialized services designate a variety of activities. Many examples can be mentioned here. To begin with there are the so called 'intermediaries': services that make available to users the skills of computer professionals. Software houses advise and assist in the development of dedicated hard- and software. Consultancy bureaus offer organizational advice in manufacturing and office automation projects. Bureaus aimed at small firms offer legal advice and perform contracted computer operations. It is also possible to hire computer facilities on a part time basis. The instruction of computer users is carried out by special training institutes. The computer manuals and course material which they use are developed by special 'manual service' bureaus, or by free lance writers working for publishers. The computer camp is a new phenomenon, which facilitates both learning to use a computer as well as the usual recreational activities.

c. For the marketing of microcomputers and software, including all related activities, computer fairs have played an important role. The distribution of software packages is mainly carried out by computer shops, mail order businesses and publishers, though producers often sell direct to the public.

2. Although commercial *computer networks,* such as Telenet,

Tymnet and Uninet are still used mainly by large enterprises (Lockheed and SDC together take up about 70% of all the so called 'information retrieval business' in the USA), network applications are ripe for exploitation by smaller firms. At present the networks offer possibilities for transmission of actual news, or to open databases for international users. Lockheed, for example, offers the DIALOG-system with hundreds of databases with millions of records. This system is accessible via various commercial networks. When the number of network users increases it will become more attractive for producers to publish in electronic form. At the moment, financial newsletters are the main type of electronic publication. The most important users of database services are large enterprises and educational and government institutions. The possibilities for 'computer conferencing' are also very promising. This is an extremely flexible way of enabling people to confer since they do not have to be in the same place nor communicating at the same time. In combination with video apparatus the possibility of 'teleconferences' arises. This could be used in education, training and business meetings. Although the market for services via databases is fairly concentrated at the moment, there are significant possibilities for small firms and entrepreneurs in this field. In fact, the variety of services which could possibly be offered is virtually unlimited. What is more, the capital required to make services available via commercial networks is relatively modest.

3. *Microprocessors* form the third important technological basis for new business activities. At the moment, the most important applications are in security monitoring and control systems. Several companies market security systems based on microprocessors for homes and businesses. Systems to regulate energy consumption in buildings are also available. Control systems based on microprocessors, for example in the production process, constitute a growing area for commercial development. A small firm can often compete easily with larger enterprises in this sector because they are able to develop new goods and services at much lower costs.

Conclusion

As well as displacing workers, information technology creates new employment, particularly in the information sector. The growth of this sector has contributed to the trendshift in the rest of the economy: many of the firms are characterized by highly skilled, autonomous work; undifferentiated organizations; and custom tailored products. In the future, little would seem to prevent a further growth of this sector. In the USA a yearly growth of around 40% is expected in the sales of microsoftware and microcomputers. The possibilities for the development of software are in fact only bounded by the creative capabilities of the programmers.

10. Summary

In this part we have discussed the impact of information technology on the quantity and quality of work, on organizational structure, and on products. We have examined if, and to what extent, this impact differs from that of technological innovation in the past. Our findings strongly suggest that there is a difference.

With regard to the quantity of work, the introduction of information technology seems to accelerate the historical trend of capital intensification which is accompanied by reductions in the average numbers of hours worked per year. The other changes associated with information technology signal a *trendshift*. Degradation of work is transformed – though hesitantly – into upgrading; differentiation and increasing scale into reintegration and decreasing scale; and mass production into custom tailored production. The rise of the information sector has reinforced this trendshift. On the micro level, firms that implement information technology accordingly are likely to gain an edge over their competitors.

The future with information technology will present unique opportunities for further socio-technological innovation of our firms. However, it may also be applied in the traditional manner, guided by the conventional wisdom of the industrial past. Under this scenario innovation is conceived as a purely technological problem. Such a limited approach would not only endanger our competitive edge, but also undermine the innovative potential of Western economies. This conclusion is strongly reinforced by our findings regarding the socio-cultural changes of Western societies to which we will turn next.

Part IV: Individualization: the megatrend

Not only technological change, but also the related process of social change has undergone a historically unique acceleration in the post war period. To get an insight into the direction of this change, we shall first briefly consider a few of the 'classic' social scientists whose characterizations of modern societies – developed in the early years of this century – have lost but little of their significance. Their observations can be reduced to one and the same major trend: the individualization or differentiation of Western culture. The present informatization of society appears to considerably accelerate this process (chapter 11). The high rate of individualization is expressed by changes in work orientation (chapter 12), in organizational strategies (chapter 13), and in consumer preference (chapter 14). These changes present a unique challenge to the business world. As will be further examined in part V, the response to this challenge must be sought in accelerated social innovation to which – as appeared in part III – information technology is particularly suited.

11. Informatization and individualization

A highly influential characterization of the evolution of Western societies since the Industrial Revolution can be found in the work of the French sociologist Emile Durkheim (1858–1917).[1] Like the founder of economics, Adam Smith, Durkheim regards the division of work as the central force behind this evolution. Whereas Adam Smith concentrated mainly on the growth of productivity, Durkheim, about a century later, considered the division of work to be the driving force behind increasing cultural differentiation, i.e. individualization. Pre-industrial society is relatively strongly integrated; collectively accepted norms and values determine individual behaviour. In Durkheim's terminology: the 'conscience collective' and the 'conscience individuelle' coincide. Division of work disrupts this homogeneity and leads to the disintegration of society. The social cohesion weakens, norm differentiation and deviant behaviour increase. This is expressed, amongst other things, by the secularization of society.

Durkheim recognized the pre-eminent integrating function of religion. Secularization meant an attack on religion-supported 'conscience collective'. Like Ivan Karamasow, the agnostic Durkheim asked himself: 'Once God is dead, does not everything become permissible?'. His view of the cohesive function of religion can be paraphrased as follows. Without relationships with his fellow men, man cannot maintain himself. In fact, man is existentially dependant on the society in which he lives, even though he often may not be aware of this. In religion the power of society over the individual is projected onto a transcendental Supreme Being. Obedience to the 'conscience collective' and obedience to God coincide. 'God is society', or rather its symbolic representation. Individualization, secularization, and disintegration form – sociologically viewed – a trio, which summarizes the modernization of Western culture.

Max Weber (1864–1920)[2] analyzed the individualization of Western culture from another angle. Central to Weber's analysis is the 'Entzauberung der Welt': the rationalization or demystification of society. The natural sciences replace the traditional under-pinnings of man's place in the universe. The process of 'Ent-zauberung' detaches him from the collective-mystical experience of reality, as appears from the replacement of Catholicism by the more personal and demystified Protestantism. The Protestant moral (the 'Innerweltliche Askese') explains, according to Weber, why the West, and not the East, took the lead in indus-trialization and economic growth.

Applied to the production organization, Weber sees a shift taking place from patronage and loyalty relations to a more business like approach with well defined rights and duties. In this he sees the rise of the modern bureaucracy which, from the standpoint of efficiency, he regards as a positive development. Compared to traditional forms, the bureaucratic organization reacts fast and efficiently to changes. It contains, still according to Weber, a superiority comparable to that of a machine. It regulates human activities according to rational goal-means relationships. (In Weber's time individualization and bureaucratization went together. Nowadays these trends are directly opposing, and with regard to bureaucratization, a trendshift can be observed. We shall return to this point in chapter 13.)

Already present in the work of Durkheim and Weber, yet more explicit in the modern literature, is a trend which is related to individualization and 'Entzauberung': that of emancipation/de-mocratization of society. The declining legitimation of social inequality may be connected to the process of secularization (Beteille, 1969), but can also be related to the industrialization process (Kerr et al., 1960; Goldthorpe, 1970). Beteille summar-izes: 'Everywhere there seems to have come about a steady erosion in the legitimacy accorded to social inequality. If social inequality continues to exist as a fact, it is no longer accepted by all as a part of the natural order, but is challenged, or at least questioned, at every point (. . .) the decline in the legitimacy of social inequality is perhaps the most important feature of the nineteenth and twentieth centuries'.[3]

The various views of the classical sociologists with regards to the evolution of Western culture can, in essence, be traced back to one and the same major trend: the individualization or differentiation of Western society. This macro trend can also be observed on the micro level: individual and society evolve in parallel, though not always in a straight line. The rise of Fascism in the 1930s for example shows how individual and society can collectively regress, and reverse the process of 'individualization-de-mystification-emancipation' by (temporarily) embracing a pre-individualistic delusion as the solution to all problems. Weber, by the way, was well aware of this when he wrote: 'The many (demystified) Gods from the past, rise from their graves, strive towards power over our lives and start once again their eternal battle amongst each other'.[4] Also at present – whether or not induced by the economic recession – signs of regression can be observed, amongst other things in the form of authoritarian, individuality absorbing sects and movements. These, and other signs of regression, are indicative of the adjustment problems society has to cope with in a time of accelerated individualization.

Individualization in the information society

Modern society is characterized by increasing 'informatization', in the sense of intensification and diversification of information and communication. The computer and telecommunication technology continually accelerate this process, and the end is not yet in sight. The explosive growth of information is shown in the most diverse areas. For example, in the technological field, 80,000 reports appeared in the USA in 1980 alone. In the world as a whole 8000 scientific articles appeared each working day – an increase of 5000 compared to 1965. The growing *overinformation,* not only in science and technology but in practically every other field as well, forces each member of society to adopt (complexity reducing) selection criteria. New to this is not the selection process as such – which takes place in any society – but the inappropriateness of traditional criteria internalized in childhood and during education. As a result, everybody has to invent (and continually renew) his own criteria, and create (and continually renew) his own reality. The informatization of society therefore accelerates the historical trend of individualization and cultural differentiation. This is clearly seen by Toffler:

> Instead of merely receiving our mental model of reality, we are now compelled to invent it and continually reinvent it (...) Caught up in that effort, we develop a heightened awareness of our own individuality of the traits that make us unique. Our self image thus changes (...) The communications revolution gives us each a more complex image of our self. It differentiates us further.[5]

From a philisophical point of view the effect of overinformation can be illustrated by (a variant of) Plato's cave myth. In this myth Plato imagines the human race to be a group of people chained together in a cave. Because of the light (fire) outside the cave, they see shadows moving on the cave wall. Shadows provide information about the reality outside the cave, but do not coincide with that reality. However, being tied to their chains, the people are not able to distinguish shadow from reality. Not even when one of them is freed, and tells them about the world outside do they comprehend the distinction. When he continually asserts that their 'reality' is an illusion, they eventually become so angry that they kill him (the person meant is Plato's teacher Socrates).

With this myth Plato shows himself to be a classical philosopher in the sense that he believes in an absolute truth: information concerning reality outside the cave. In the information society this belief is continually losing ground. The process of informatization does not just put one person, but every person outside the cave. In the 'real' world they are confronted by so many, and moreover such diverse 'truths', that each of them comes up with his own selection and his own reality. In other words, the cave people have become individualized, thereby discovering the relative meaning of their own 'reality', i.e. the shadow character of *all* information. In this process even Socrates becomes 'entzaubert', and is no longer threatening. His reality also appears to be a personal, subjective choice from all available information and is therefore equal to that of others. Individualization, 'Entzauberung', and emancipation can thus be considered as interdependant consequences of the process of informatization.

Statistical evidence to support the individualization of Western culture is extremely limited. Time series of social indicators, in particular for the pre-war period, are not available. The statistical material shows gaps, and is inconsistent, because during the course of time new definitions and categories have regularly been adopted. Nevertheless, a few indicators can be constructed from 1900 onwards.

From a theoretical standpoint, several indicators are appropriate. Individualization is accompanied by a decline of social control and social cohesion. Opportunities for self actualization increase, but so does the chance of disorientation and dislocation. The available indicators mainly illustrate this last aspect. Durkheim, for example, took suicide as an indicator of individualization and noted a positive correlation. Other indicators of social cohesion are, for example, the rate of criminality, divorce, tax fraud, refusal to do military service, etc. Only the first two – crime and divorce – are available in the form of internationally comparable time series (from 1900, corrected for population increase). Both indicators, reproduced in figures 11.1. and 11.2., show an almost identical pattern for all countries. After a gradual increase in the period before the Second World War, the post-war period from the second half of the 1960s onwards shows an explosive acceleration. The rates have at least trebled in all countries (apart from the divorce rate in the USA; which is due to the relatively high initial rate in the 1960s).

An additional determinant of the currently high rates could be the destabilizing effect of the acceleration as such. Post-war society is experiencing, in the words of Alvin Toffler, a 'Future Shock'.[6] Existing norms and institutions are transforming at an extremely high rate, and individuals are unable to adapt. Before the Second World War this rate was much lower and we were not therefore put to any great test. It is not, by the way, easy to distinguish the effect of the individualization process as such from the effect of the acceleration of this process. We shall adopt the hypothesis that increased disintegration of society is the common result of both determinants.

To illustrate the Weberian 'Entzauberung' – the rationalization of society – several indicators are useful: research and development

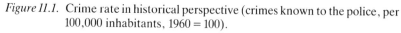

Figure 11.1. Crime rate in historical perspective (crimes known to the police, per 100,000 inhabitants, 1960 = 100).

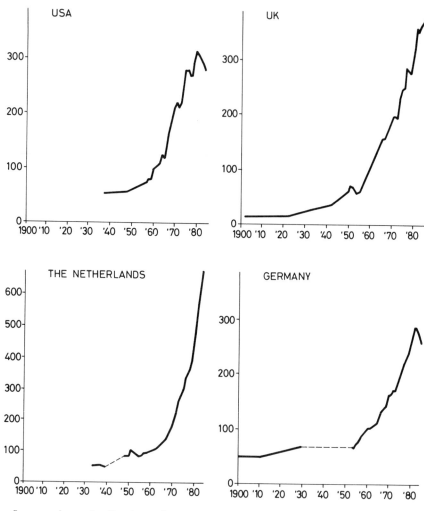

Source and remarks: See Appendix.

expenses, patent applications, scientific publications, student numbers. Especially important is the indicator of technological innovation: the capital intensity of the production process (already shown in figure 4.1.). Time series from 1900 are only available for the number of students (corrected for population increase, figure 11.3.). The graphs are virtually identical to the previous ones: after a gradual rise from 1900, the post-war period

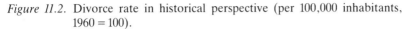

Figure 11.2. Divorce rate in historical perspective (per 100,000 inhabitants, 1960 = 100).

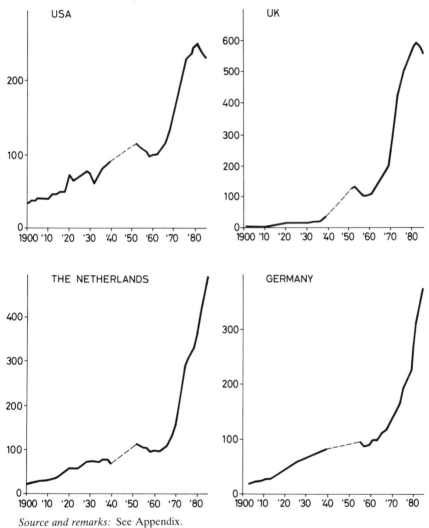

Source and remarks: See Appendix.

from the second half of the 1960s onwards shows an unprecedented acceleration.

As an indicator of the emancipation of society, a disaggregation of the number of students (by sex and class) could be used. However, the statistical material is insufficient, as is true for other indicators: participation of women in the labour market, social

Figure 11.3. Tertiary schooling in historical perspective (students per 1000 in-
       habitants, 1960 = 100).

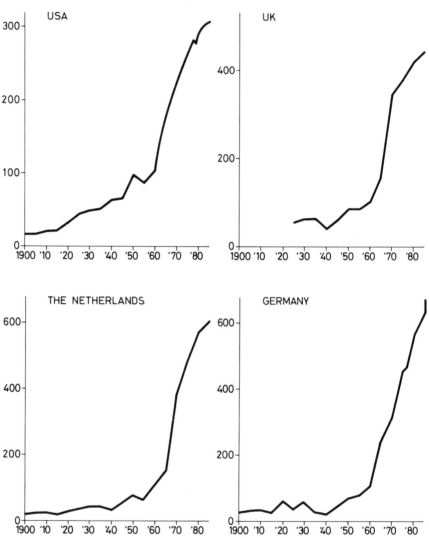

Source and remarks: See Appendix.

mobility, income equality, etc. As a proxy for emancipation,
however, the share of social security payments in the national
income (figure 11.4.)[7] is available. Social security has not only
contributed to income equalization, but also to the emancipation
of economically inactive persons. Under the present legal system

Figure 11.4. Social security expenditures in historical perspective (in percentages of gross domestic product).

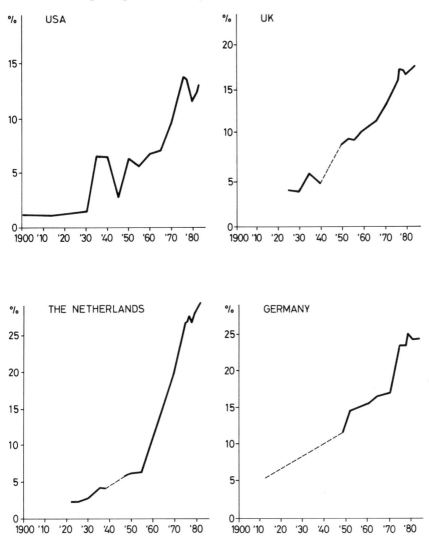

Source and remarks: See Appendix.

at least, social security payments offer an acceptable indicator of the emancipation process. The pattern – though not traceable for all countries from 1900 – is the same as that of the other earlier indicators, with once again a post-war acceleration.

The previous analysis leads to the following conclusions:
– The evolution of Western society in the last centuries can be characterized as a process of individualization and/or differentiation (accompanied by increasing 'Entzauberung' and emancipation).
– Under the influence of the informatization of society, the individualization process has accelerated (from around the second half of the 1960s) to an unprecedented rate.
– Time series of a number of social indicators confirm this historically unique acceleration. It should be remarked here that this acceleration shows a striking similarity with that of the technological innovation shown in figure 4.1. This similarity seems to confirm the interdependant character of the two.

It is difficult to predict the consequences of further overinformation and individualization in the near future. Chances are that social cohesion will be further weakened, which could further endanger the governability of society. A minimum collective consciousness is a precondition to collect taxes, prevent misuse of social security, to guarantee safety, in short, to allow democracy to function. In the future this minimum may not be realized unless we bring society's institutions in line with the individualization trend. For the time being, the growing overinformation will tend to diminish the transparency of society rather than increase it. This problem is subtely illustrated by the last verse of T.S. Eliots 'Choruses from the Rock':
> Where is the wisdom we have lost in knowledge?
> Where is the knowledge we have lost in information?

For the business world the informatization/individualization trend presents an unknown challenge as will become evident in the following chapters.

12. The changing work orientation: not more but better

Individualization is expressed in the norms and attitudes of society. In this chapter we shall concentrate on the changes in work attitudes. For some time the traditional Puritan work ethic appears to give way to an orientation that emphasizes skilled, autonomous work, i.e. one that eschews the routine work characteristic of the classical factory. This change in work orientation, on the supply side of the labour market, will appear to dovetail with the changes on the demand side noted in chapter 6.

> Yankelovich, Skelly & White Inc., a New York consulting company that has studied employee attitudes in the workplace for 13 years has tracked a slow but steady drift away from traditional work values, which are based on the Puritan work ethic and the belief that it is intrinsically important to work. Instead, increasing numbers of people are adopting new values that stress the importance of personal satisfaction and the ability to learn from their work. (...) Fulfillment-oriented people are looking to achieve, to learn more, to grow (...) Already 40% of the US work force has adopted at least some of the new values and that group is growing every year. (Business Week, February 20, 1984.)

Yankelovich's research is one of an increasing number of studies on the changes in work orientation. These changes are not independant of the trend toward individualization, but form an integral part of it. They may also be connected to the rising level of education and/or the increased standard of living, i.e. to developments running parallel with the individualization trend.

In the 'Interfutures' report from the OECD[1] a great deal of

attention is paid to post-war cultural changes and their consequences for the Western economies. Inspired by a book of the
same name by Inglehart[2], the OECD report argues that a 'silent
revolution' is taking place in which modern, post-materialistic
values are replacing traditional, materialistic values. This transformation is explained by the fact that (1) in almost all OECD
countries primary living requirements are guaranteed for every
citizen, and (2) the degree of schooling has increased sharply
(described as 'cognitive mobilization'). Post materialism is characterized in general by 'an increasing concern for individual self-
expression', and in the factory by 'workers demands for re-
organization of the assembly line into smaller, more autonomous
groups in which each member has a voice in how the job is done'.
The desire for self actualization and autonomy is accompanied by
'a dissatisfaction with traditional hierarchically structured bureaucratic forms of organization. Demands for a more egalitarian
style of decision-making (. . .) may reflect an increasing emphasis
on the desire to be a full member of whatever unit occupies one's
working hours, and to express oneself as a person not simply a
hired hand'.[3] The new work-orientation is conceived as a consequence of improved living standards, which, in turn, correlates
with the long-term trend toward individualization.

In management circles the reintegration of work tasks is often
considered to be incompatible with efficiency. In an earlier
OECD report, 'Policies for life at work' (1977), this Tayloristic
idea is put to the test as an old fashioned prejudice. The report
notes a 'gradual accumulation of research and experience showing that optimal job-life can contribute to efficiency, either directly in production or indirectly through lower labour turnover
and absence, and improved commitment and teamwork. The
trend is clearly towards more and more managers recognizing that
a good joblife is simply good business.'[4]

In a report by the Dutch Scientific Council for Government
Policy (SCGP)[5] the diagram reproduced in figure 12.1. is used to
illustrate the changing attitudes towards work. This diagram confirms the trend pointed out by the OECD. The increasing standard of living and rising level of education, together with the
accompanying emancipation, have led to increased demand for
higher quality work. In another report also published in 1977,

Figure 12.1. Determinants of the changing work attitudes as seen by the Dutch
        SCGP.

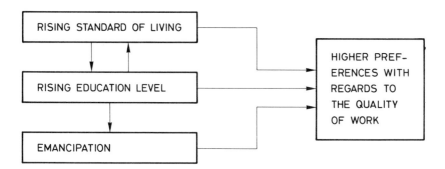

'The next twenty five years',[6] the Council notes a link between the changing work orientation and the secularization of society. The 'duty ethic' associated with religious practise is being replaced by a more worldly 'self actualization ethic'. Surveys in the area of work orientation in Germany[7], the USA[8] and Sweden[9] all indicate changes in the same direction.

Summarizing, it can be said that there has recently been a notable change in work-orientation in Western countries. The demand for work which requires high qualifications, autonomy and creativity is increasing.

The changing work-orientation on the supply side of the labour market reinforces the change on the demand side noted in chapter 6. Figure 12.2. gives an idealized view of both developments from the 1950s. The decreasing demand for higher qualified work in the industrial age reverses in a slight increase around 1970. The increased preference for this work is reproduced in the supply curve which rises slowly before and rapidly after 1970. From the 1950s onwards, demand and supply appear to show an increasing discrepancy. After 1970, this discrepancy has (probably) continued to increase slightly, despite the trendshift on the demand side of the labour market. Demand is lagging behind the changing work orientation on the supply side. The jobs offered fall short with repect to the quality of work which employees consider appropriate. The consequence is twofold:

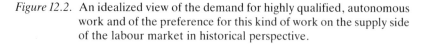

Figure 12.2. An idealized view of the demand for highly qualified, autonomous work and of the preference for this kind of work on the supply side of the labour market in historical perspective.

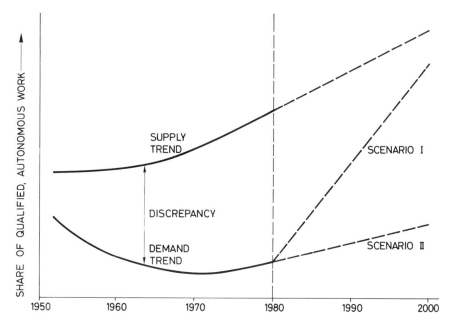

- From the employee's viewpoint, the discrepancy has contributed to declining work satisfaction, particularly in the 1960s and 1970s, which contributed to a high rate of both sick leave and turnover in personel.[10]
- From the employer's viewpoint, there has been a decline in efficiency. During the last ten years the competitive edge of Western firms has declined more than necessary due to an increasing under-utilization of 'human resources'.

The prognosis for the remainder of this century is captured in the following two scenario's. Assuming that the preference for quality work – parallel to the individualization trend – will continue to increase, (indicated in figure 12.2. by a dotted line) these two scenarios can be characterized as follows:

- Scenario I: Social innovation is regarded as a precondition for successful technological innovation: the opportunities offered by information technology for an improvement in the quality of work are optimally utilized. (The inseparable changes in the organization of firms will be dealt with in the following chapter.)

– Scenario II: 'Conventional wisdom' guides technological innovation. The discrepancy between demand and supply in the labour market increases (or at least does not decrease): the Western competitive edge will further erode.

Conclusion

1. The individualization of society is accompanied by an increasing preference for higher quality work (an increasing desire for self actualization and autonomy in work). In the future, it can be assumed that this trend will continue due to further informatization/individualization of society.

2. Although information technology may recently have improved the quality of work, this improvement has lagged behind changing preferences on the supply side of the labour market.

3. Information technology can and should be utilized to remove this discrepancy, which would also strengthen the competitive edge of our economy.

13. The end of Taylorism

Organizational changes can be brought about by both technological and social factors (see chapter 7). In this chapter we will deal with the second category, in particular with the long-term changes in strategies and attitudes concerning the most efficient organizational structure. These changes will be related to the impact of information technology on the organization of firms discussed in chapter 7.

As noted earlier Max Weber characterized the evolution of Western culture in terms of 'Entzauberung', i.e. rationalization and demystification of society. Traditional feudal 'production organizations' went through a process of bureaucratization, characterized by, according to Weber, a rigid division and prescription of tasks and competence, formal hierarchy and fixed rules.

As an exponent of the same rationalization trend, Frederick Taylor (1911) developed his so-called 'Scientific Management'. Through systematic observation of workers, work relationships, and work movements (time and motion studies), Taylor worked out production methods in which all excess operations and arbitrary decisions were removed from the shop floor. Control needed to be as strict as possible, as only then could maximum efficiency be achieved:

> Workers who are only controlled by way of general orders and disciplinary rules are not controlled adequately, because they retain their hold on the work process. As long as they control their work they may frustrate attempts to fully utilize their productive potential. To change this, control of the work process must be taken over by management, not only in a formal sense, but also in the sense of dictation of every step of the process, including the way in which it is carried out.[1]

Taylor himself summarized 'Scientific Management' in the following three principles:
1. managers should exert themselves to collect all the knowledge and skill on the shop floor, and this knowledge should then be classified, tabulated, and reduced to rules, laws and formulas;
2. no mental work should take place on the shop floor, but should be removed to planning and layout departments;
3. managers should plan every worker's task at least one day in advance. In most cases every man should receive full written instructions, describing in detail what he has to do, how he has to do it, and how long he should take to do it.

The first principle encourages the process of 'deskilling' mentioned earlier and the accompanying horizontal differentiation. The second concerns the division between thinking and doing: vertical differentiation. The third indicates the necessity of managerial control as a result of (1) and (2). Taylor was, by the way, convinced that his scientific approach would benefit workers as well as improve productivity and efficiency. The negative effect on work content was a necessary sacrifice for a good cause.

The first doubts about the effectiveness of the Tayloristic model arose shortly before the Second World War after the famous experiments in the Hawthorne factory of the Western Electric Company. The result of these experiments (concerning the effects of working conditions on productivity) was that not the conditions, but primarily the social cohesion among employees determined productivity.[2] These results induced the start of a new movement in organization theory: the 'Human Relations' school. The views of this school differed strongly from Taylorism:
1. organizations must be seen primarily as a complex of social relations;
2. the 'informal' structure is at least equally important to the functioning of an organization as the formal Tayloristic structure;
3. alongside material rewards social gratifications are important in work.

The acknowledgement of the worker as a social being came – not

by chance – at a time when the emancipation of society simultaneously showed itself in many areas. It was not until long after
the Second World War, however, that a serious breach in the
belief in Tayloristic principles actually occurred.

Attempts to adapt production organizations to the aspirations and
capabilities of workers are connected with the names of Herzberg[3]
and Maslow[4] whose ideas started to gain acceptance during the
1970s. Both authors feel that in contrast to the Tayloristic view,
man has a deeply rooted desire for self actualization. To analyze
this desire Hertzberg developed the concept of *job enrichment,* in
which task elements from a qualitatively higher level are added to
existing jobs. The process of vertical differentiation, characteristic of the industrial past, is thus reversed. Control and performance are reintegrated. Alongside 'job enrichment' there is also *job
enlargement.* Differentiated tasks from the same level are reintegrated. The number of operations per worker increases. Job
enlargement is in fact the reverse of horizontal differentiation. As
a third element, we should mention *job rotation* in which workers
exchange jobs. This also implies an element of reintegration. The
three together are known as 'job design', or as 'new forms of work
organization'.[5] They have in common the two-sided recognition
that:
– the Tayloristic view of a production organization is obsolete;
– division of work, which previously promoted efficiency, now
   impedes it.

Job design, and its extension – (semi) autonomous groups –
therefore not only increases the social acceptability of work, but
also it's productivity. At this crucial point the individualization/
rationalization of society, on the one hand, and increasing bureaucratic efficiency, on the other, no longer develop in parallel.
In McCrae's words: 'the world is probably drawing to the end of
the era of big business corporations, because it would soon be
seen to be nonsense to have hierarchical managements trying to
arrange how brainworkers (who in the future will be a growing
majority) can best use their imaginations'.[6] Frustration builds up
where this process does not take place rapidly enough. Under
favourable circumstances this may lead to a new entrepreneurship

which McCrae calls 'intrapreneurship' (the internal contracting of work to autonomous groups),[7] and also to the remarkable increase in the 'one person business' described as 'the final complete worker participation, a form of self expression. The dramatic growth in self employment shows that self employment is a positive trend in society, profoundly desired by ... people who want to be their own masters, and to control their own lives'.[8]

Despite all the initiatives aimed at de-Taylorization, it must nevertheless be noted that the decisive step in this development is hardly ever taken. For this, it is necessary to realize that information technology is eminently suitable as a vehicle for the social innovation of the organization (see chapter 7 and 20). Managers should be made aware that such an integration of technological and social innovation will support the competitive edge of their firms, not temporarily but structurally.

Conclusion

1. Efforts to maximize efficiency have in the past led to an increasing Taylorization of firms.

2. The recently accelerated individualization of Western societies is incompatible with a Tayloristic organization structure. Taylorism may have improved efficiency in the past, but thwarts it now. CEOs increasingly allow individuals and groups more autonomy as this contributes to the company's performance (e.g. intrapreneurship).

3. The initiatives taken to de-Taylorize firms pay insufficient attention to the opportunities information technology has to offer. A further exploitation of these opportunities is a crucial precondition for preserving a competitive edge.

14. The individualistic consumer

This chapter deals with the influence of the individualization trend on consumer demand. The trend seems responsible for a reorientation in preferences away from mass products toward more diversified products. This reorientation could only begin to show itself when the standard of living had risen to a sufficient level. As explained in chapter 8, information technology has made it possible for firms to satisfy the diversification of demand.

The transformation of society after the Industrial Revolution also affected the relationship between producer and consumer. In the pre-industrial era both were one and the same person, or knew each other personally. Due to the fact that production was almost exclusively made-to-measure – the technology at that time left no other choice – the client could himself determine the specific characteristics of his product. Industrialization changed all this. The rise of the factory was accompanied by mass production for the market, replacing direct exchange by remote, anonymous exchange. True enough, the consumer still determined – at least according to the economic theory of consumer sovereignty – the allocation of production, but products were no longer geared to individual preferences. The re-individualization of consumer demand once again became apparent when, as a result of increasing mass production, the standard of living for the vast majority rose above subsistence level. The parallel increasing concern for self expression (see chapter 12) included a change in the consumer's taste. Uniform patterns, characteristic of the industrial past, were increasingly rejected. This new trend can be observed not only in the diversification of material goods, but also in the increasing demand for individualized services. In The Netherlands for example, mention can be made of an individualization of the social security system, and of the growing popularity of individualized education. In the future it can be expected that the individualization/diversification trend will continue as a consequence of the further informatization of society. The OECD observes that 'Expectations with regards to information technology's potential to inform consumers include both more efficient information via noncommercial information providers, i.e. consumer organizations and similar institutions, and an improvement of the information character of the majority of commercial messages which the systems will have to carry to be economically viable'.[1]

The consequence of the increasing standard of living and the individualization of society for consumer preferences were seen early by the business world. Already in 1963 Weiss published a report, for the advertising bureau Doyle Dane Bernbach Inc., entitled 'The rising tide of individual taste' in which it was stated that the improved standard of living would lead to: '. . . an upgrading in taste that will demand from manufacturers a still greater degree of individuality in design. The differences among people will become exciting. Differences in looks and dress, as well as differences in ways of thinking and living . . .'.[2]

In response to the noted individualization tendency, the business world developed a 'marketing concept'. This concept involves, amongst other things, the adoption of a more consumer-oriented approach in terms of growing consumer research, and the application of this research in product differentiation and market segmentation. Critics point out that the results often meant nothing more than the introduction of trivial differences and marginal changes in models and packaging. Toffler tones down this criticism: 'The fast increasing variety of goods and services in the high technology nations is often explained away as an attempt by the corporation to manipulate the consumer, to invent false needs, and to inflate profits by charging a lot for trivial options. No doubt, there is truth to these charges. Yet something deeper is at work. For the growing differentiation of goods and services also reflects the growing diversity of actual needs, values, and life styles in a de-massified society'.[3]

It is precisely the application of information technology in flexible production automation and computer networks which nowadays makes it possible to react adequately to the changes in consumer orientation. 'The rising tide of individual taste', which Weiss foresaw, coincided at that time with the early form of (rigid) automation, justified by its potential to continually produce larger volumes of uniform products more efficiently. After this however, flexible production automation made it possible to make both ever smaller batches and even individualized products in a profitable way. In the service sector, more powerful computers linked together in computer networks fostered a similar trend (see chapter 8).

Conclusion

1. Parallel to the cultural changes in society as a whole, consumer preferences have recently shown a trend towards individualization and diversification. The further informatization of society in the future may well stimulate this trend.

2. On the supply side of the market the application of information technology in flexible production automation and computer networks offers firms the chance to react adequately to this trend.

15. The informal economy as an escape

Until now we have limited ourselves to economic activities which are registered in statistics. However, economic reality is broader than the official statistics suggest. The part which remains unregistered is known as the informal economy. In the information society, the significance of the informal economy may well increase under the influence of both technological and social changes.

In this chapter the emphasis will be on the so-called 'white' part of the informal economy. This part includes 'all activities which hardly differ from officially recognized professional work, but for which no financial rewards are offered in compensation, and for which laws and social security legislation are not applicable (for example housework, voluntary work, do-it-yourself.)'[1] These activities should be distinguished from the 'black' part of the informal economy such as tax fraud and other underground activities. The white informal economy often requires skilled labour, takes place in small organizations, and produces custom tailored products. The rise of these activities in the 70s and 80s may be seen as a reinforcement of the trendshift in Western economies.

In the past, the industrialization of the Western world was accompanied by the disappearance of all kinds of home-work and self-service, or by the accommodation of these in the formal (market) economy. Industrialization and formalization were two sides of the same coin. As Gershuny puts it: 'In the two centuries since Adam Smith's birth, the aggregate effect (. . .) has been the great transformation from household and communal production to formal industrial production'.[2] The decline of the industrial sector around 1970 heralded the start of the post-industrial society. The so-called tertiary or service sector took over. However, part of the growth of the service sector took place outside the formal economy: the post-industrial society was accompanied by a revival of the informal economy.

Taking a look at the literature, the economist Feige considers the informal sector to be: 'all economic activities of government and individuals which as a result of accountancy conventions, under-reporting of income, avoidance of social registration, lead to them not being processed as (gross) national income in National Accounts'.[3] Feige has calculated the development of this 'invisible monetary sector' in the USA and the UK for the period 1960 – 1979 (see figure 15.1.). Not only the absolute size, but also the growth rate of this sector is remarkable: in both countries there has been a more than sixfold increase in the 1970s (not corrected for inflation).

Another way of mapping the informal sector is by way of time allocation patterns. Examples of this approach can be found in Gershuny and the Dutch Social and Cultural Report of 1982. Gershuny defines the informal economy as: 'an economy based on the non-money production of services within the household', but also as '(an economy which) contains a diverse collection of activities that may be divided into three categories: the household, the communal and the underground. This last in turn covers a wide range, from outright theft, to tax evasion and moonlighting'.[4] On the basis of 2400 diaries kept by respondants, he has made a table showing how time was spent each day in the UK in

Table 15.1. Results of Gershuny's research into time spending patterns.

	hours per day	
	1961	1974/5
Out-of-home		
– work	4.2	3.7
– other	1.8	1.9
Home		
– housework	2.3	3.0
– passive recreation	2.4	2.4
– other	13.4	13.0

Source: J. Gershuny, The informal economy, *Futures*, Feb. 1979, p. 13.

Figure 15.1. Estimate of the size of the invisible monetary sector in the USA and
            UK, 1960–1979.

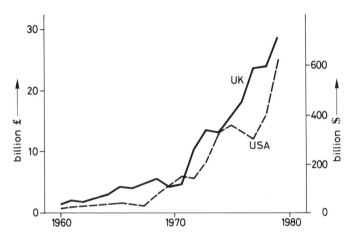

Source: Feige, E.L., The UK's unobserved economy: a preliminary assessment, *The
        Journal of Economic Affairs*, July 1981.

two periods (in 1961 and 1974/5, see table 15.1.). From these
statistics it appears that the category 'work' has declined by at
least 10%, while 'house work' has risen by a good 30%. Gershuny:
'The proportion of time spent working for money appears to have
declined over the period, whilst the time devoted to the informal
production of services has increased'.[5] The research does not give
any definite answer to the question whether or not this shift has
taken place gradually over the period, or – as with Feige – first
occurs after 1970. Statistics from the Netherlands indicate that this
shift has also continued after 1975 (see Table 15.2., column 3).

Table 15.2. Formal and informal work in the Netherlands 1975–1980
            (in thousands of working years).

	1975	1980	1980/1975 × 100
Formal work	4443	4584	103
Informal work	6463	7320	113
– of which do-it-yourself	966	1397	145

Source: Calculated from the Dutch SCR 1982, p. 66.

There are various explanations of the growth in the informal economy. Limiting ourselves to the white part, a number of technological and social-cultural factors can be distinguished.

The influence of technology may be summarized in two major themes. As a spin-off of post-war, technological development, a collection of tools and materials has been created which can be utilized by everyone. This self service by the consumer may be described as disintermediation, i.e. as a reduction of the distance between producer and consumer. Secondly, technological innovation was accompanied by a continuous decline in formal working hours (see chapter 5), i.e. the rise of leisure time, as a result of which more time was created for forms of self production. In the same way that technological innovation in the industrial era led to formalization, now in the post-industrial era it leads to informalization of economic activities. In 1975 Burns described this trend-shift as follows: 'It was our capacity for a series of technological advances that brought about an abrupt and radical shift in the balance between the household and market economies, a shift that has now reached maturity and is, of itself, reversing'.[6]

The effect of technological innovation is strengthened by social-cultural changes. First, the shift in work-orientation (see chapter 12) fits well into the organizational setting of the informal economy. According to Miles, it is precisely the informal economy which offers the chance 'to find useful work to do, and furthermore to work autonomously, free of regulations of large corporations and the alienation of the mass market mechanisms'.[7] Other factors, such as ecological motives, cost considerations, etc. may also play a role.

A further growth of the informal economy is likely in the future. New information and communication technologies accompanied by further cultural changes will stimulate this growth. According to the EEC report, 'Forecasting and Assessment in the field of Science and Technology (FAST)', the following three factors will have a great impact on the economy of the information society:
   – the spread of the tertiary sector;
   – new technological opportunities;
   – new relationships between the so-called formal economy and informal or non-market activities.[8]

The continuing growth of the service sector offers new growth possibilities for the informal or 'self service' economy. Information technology strengthens this development because (1) it creates more advanced tools and new forms of do-it-yourself work; (2) because working hours in the formal economy will be further reduced; and (3) because the 'marriage' between information and communication technologies decouples formal activities from time and place. This could lead to a revival of home-work and to a weakening of the boundary between formal and informal work.

The American research bureau, Arthur D. Little, foresees in their report 'The Netherlands in the Information Age' the creation of decentralized networks and greater flexibility in the location and scheduling of work. They conclude that these developments point to 'a reintegration of work and family life'.[9] Added to a strong tendency toward individualization, this reintegration could eventually result in Toffler's 'prosumer-society'[10], in which producer and consumer are more and more reunited. For the time being, however, we must make do with the conclusion that *informatization leads to informalization* and that therefore a further growth of the informal economy can be expected.

This informal economy should not by the way be perceived as a threat, but as complementary to the formal economy. Contrary to the past, the formal economy is not a substitute for the informal economy but forms the basis for it. In the formal economy the production of intermediary goods takes place – mainly in automated form – whereas final production mainly takes place in the informal economy. In Gershuny's words:

– Final production takes place increasingly in the home, while work outside the home is more and more concerned with intermediate production of the goods (...) used for the home-based final production.
– Out-of-home employment is increasingly concerned with planning and programming production; presumably with automation the number of jobs involving the direct transformation of material will decrease.[11]

Conclusion

Since around 1800 the industrialization of the economy has led to a decline of what is now often called the informal sector. During the last decades a trendshift seems to have occurred: the informal sector is growing again. Both information technology and the individualization of society have contributed to this revival. In the future, the continuing informatization of the economy can be expected to further stimulate the informalization process.

16. Summary

In this part we have discussed some social-cultural changes in our current information society. In particular, we called attention to changes relevant for the business world: the work orientation of employees, the conceptions of managers and the consumer's preferences.

On the macro level, the industrial past has shown an increasing individualization or differentiation of society. Due to the current 'informatization' this trend is accelerating. Applied to employees work orientation, the accelerated individualization shows itself in an increasing desire for self expression and autonomy, i.e. in increasing resistance to routine work. With regard to the managerial conceptions, there is a break away from Tayloristic principles which appear to be incompatible with the individualization trend. The belief is spreading that increasing the autonomy of individuals and groups contributes to the company's performance (e.g. through intrapreneurship). With regard to consumer preferences, a change can be observed from mass products to more diversified tastes. The rise of the 'white' informal economy provides further evidence of the need felt by individuals for self expression and autonomy in small-scale work environments.

These findings strongly reinforce the need for socio-technological innovation of our firms, the main conclusion of part III. Economic necessity (preserving our competitive edge), technological possibility (socio-technological innovation), and social desirability (based on changing attitudes of workers, managers and consumers) all point in the same direction. It is this convergence that provides us with a Western Edge to meet the Eastern Challenge.

Part V: The Western Edge

In this final part we shall begin by taking a closer look at the country which during the last decades not only astounded friend and foe with its rapid economic growth, but even threatens to outdo the West in some vital branches of industry: Japan. The Japanese phenomenon is a more than obvious one to consider as nowadays a large number of Western firms are trying to introduce a Japanese style culture in order to improve their results. This imitation puts the cart before the horse. The appropriate 'Western innovation' will be profiled against this background.

17. Misguided lessons from Japan

In 1982 the number of industrial robots in Japan was more than double that of the USA, treble that of Germany, and more than in all Atlantic countries together.[1] The rapid robotization of Japanese industry is indicative of the success of the Japanese economy as a whole during the last decades. During the 60s this success was convincingly shown by the extremely high growth rates which astounded many Western observers. After the oil crisis, Japan appears to be still in the lead, as can be seen in table 17.1. In the period 1973–1980 the average growth of Japan's gross national product was almost double that of growth in the USA and the EEC countries. Productivity growth shows an even sharper contrast both for the economy as a whole (with an almost zero growth in the USA), and for the industrial sector by itself. At the same time, unemployment in Japan was far below the Western average: 1.9% in Japan, compared to 6.5% in the USA, and 4.6% in the EEC.

Many are of the opinion that Japan's success is due to the specific features of the Japanese firm and/or Japanese culture in general.

Table 17.1. Average yearly GNP-growth and unemployment percentage in Japan, the USA and the EEC, 1973–1980.

	GNP (real)	Productivity*		Unemployment
		total	industry	
Japan	3.8	3.0	3.7	1.9
USA	2.1	0.1	1.7	6.5
EEC	2.2	2.2	1.5	4.6

* GNP divided by employment.

Source: Japan, Economic Surveys, OECD, July 1981, p. 37.

Illustrative of this is a 'Business Week Special Report' which appeared as early as 1978 entitled 'Texas Instruments shows US-business how to survive the eighties'. The TI directors regard the introduction of a 'Japanese style culture' in their firm as a precondition for survival. The boom in 'Lessons from Japan' literature in recent years suggest a superiority of Japanese management techniques as well. In The Netherlands one could point to the recently established MANS Foundation (Management and Work New Style, an initiative of the Employers Federation of the Metal and Electronic Industry) which tries to stimulate managers to model their firm on Japanese lines. Particularly the 'Statistical Quality Control' techniques are 'en vogue'. In order to understand why these and other techniques do work for Japan but not for us, it is important to gain some insight into the characteristic features of management and organization in Japanese firms. At least three such features – particularly characteristic of large firms – appear repeatedly in the literature.

A. 'Lifetime employment'
   Employees in large firms usually enjoy 'lifetime employment': from the moment they leave school until retirement (at age 55) they stay with the same employer. This is not a result of any law or contract, but rests on a custom which is socially sanctioned. Welfare facilities in Japan are also organized in, around, and by the firms. The expansiveness of these facilities determine the social status of an employee in society. In turn, the employee is loyal and totally dedicated to the firm. Women however, are excluded from the system of 'lifetime employment'. Around their twenty fifth year (the generally accepted marriage age) they resign and later return to the labour market only as either part-timers or as temporary employees. Small firms usually do not have the means to guarantee 'lifetime employment', but nevertheless do try to follow this culturally embedded principle.

B. 'Seniority principle'
   The Japanese firm is built on vertical relationships legitimated by all concerned. Hierarchy is the factor which counts: the members of the firm have much stronger ties with their superi-

ors than with their colleagues. Historically this vertical orientation can be traced back to the Samurai 'ie-system', traces of which can still be found in many institutions and organizations. In firms this system is expressed by the seniority principle in which age forms the basic criterion for salary and promotion: 'seniority rating' versus 'merit rating'. Compared to the West, wage differences in Japan therefore seem more disconnected from market forces.

C. 'Management by consensus'
Japanese management is known for it's emphasis on harmonious relationships in the firm (often associated with Buddhism), and the related participative decision system: 'management by consensus'. Managers and workers feel a collective responsibility for the firm which explains why certain control techniques (e.g. the statistical quality control developed in the West in the 1930s by the American statistician W. Edwards Deming) were immediately popular in Japan but resisted in the West. Statistical quality control boils down to recording all activities in the firm, including the worker's mistakes, and subsequently using these records as inputs to managerial decision-making. The Japanese worker does not see this practice as a threat to his autonomy, because basically he does not wish to consider himself as an autonomous individual (see the following chapter).

The three characteristics are closely interrelated. In fact they can all be considered as components of Japanese management philosophy, indicated by the term *keie kazoku-shugi*. This term can be translated as 'managerial familyism' or 'industrial familyism', indicating that the firm functions as a pseudo-family in the sense of an 'ie' household: a group closely linked together via vertical relationships in which the members subordinate their individual interests. It hardly needs to be argued that such an organization, more or less operating as a military unit, easily surpasses the achievements of the much less coherent Western firm. At the same time it is no less evident that its success depends foremost on the legitimation of the system by all members, i.e. on the pre-individualistic consciousness in Japanese society. For this reason the Japanese model cannot be transfered to the West. More strongly, even in Japan this model is now showing the first signs of an irreversible erosion.

18. Japanese on Japan

Japanese society differs not only in degree, but also in principle from the West. This makes it difficult to characterize Japan using a Western frame of reference. Western literature appears to be insufficiently sensitive to the specific character of Japanese culture. To do justice to this culture one must consult the Japanese literature itself.

At least two Japanese analyses of Japanese society have gained international recognition: one by the anthropologist Chie Nakane,[1] and another by the psychoanalyst Takeo Doi.[2] Nakane characterizes Japan primarily as a vertical society. The way in which institutions are organized still carries the marks of feudal Japan, in particular the vertically organized military caste: the Samurai. In Europe the feudal system has gradually disappeared since the Industrial Revolution. In Japan, however, industrialization has only recently taken place and modern technology has been more or less directly linked to feudal social patterns. According to Nakane, Japanese firms owe their internal cohesion and competitive power to precisely this vertical structure. Her analysis also explains the low frequency of industrial conflicts which Western observers often find difficult to understand. Both in the Japanese firm and in Japanese society as a whole conflicting interests are normally only conceivable with the 'outgroup': non-Japan.

   Doi's analysis is particularly enlightening because he explains the main features of Japanese culture in terms of the Freudian frame of reference which is well known to Western observers. The essence of the Japanese personality, in Doi's 'Anatonomy of Dependance', lies in 'the propensity to enter into an "amae" relationship'. For the term 'amae' (similarly for an extensive number of related terms) there is in fact no English equivalent. An 'amae' relationship can be described as a symbiotic 'basic trust' relationship between social inequals. The socially lower confesses his emotional dependance to the socially higher, who in turn shows his willingness to stand by him as a father figure. An 'amae' relation is entered into for life and is usually considered to be more important than the man-wife relationship. From a Freudian perspective, the 'amae' relation satisfies the often subconscious desire for unconditional acceptance, i.e. for 'passive love': 'the need to appease men's sense of impotence'. The price of the gratification of this need is dependancy, or in Freudian terms: the stagnation of personality development in a pre-individualistic phase. According to Doi, 'Japan has failed to establish the freedom of the individual as distinct from the group'. He ascribes the difference between Japanese and Western societal development to the different religious background. Buddhism and Shintoism, in contrast to Christianity, have no personal God. The gratification a Christian experiences in his relationship with his God (placed above society) can to a certain extent be compared with the gratification experienced in 'amae' relations (within society). Due to the bond with God, Christians do not have to rely so heavily on their fellow men. Social cohesion in Western society is therefore not as strong as in Japan. Christianity contained in other words the necessary conditions for the individualization of Western society. In Japan the representation of God remained incorporated in society and this, according to Doi, not only contributed to a strong feeling of nationalism, but also to Japan's economic success. 'The industrialization that has been carried out at such a frantic pace since Japan's defeat in the last war can be seen, similarly, as inspired by the same national motives'. Doi does, however, feel that Japan is on its way to a more individualized society: 'The propensity to enter into "amae" relations is diminishing'.

Doi feels that 'the emphasis on vertical relationships that social anthropologist Nakane Chie stipulated as characteristic of the Japanese-type social structure could also be seen as an emphasis on "amae". One might be justified, even, in seeing the susceptibility to "amae" as the cause of this emphasis on vertical relationships'.[3] Both Nakane and Doi therefore seem to be pointing at

the same roots of Japanese society, though from different per-
spectives. In fact, both focus on the pre-individualistic nature of
Japanese society, emphasizing the contrast with the individualized West. Moreover, both hold these roots to be responsible
for the booming post-war economic growth in Japan.

The difference between the West and Japan can be supported by
available statistical time series. The increasing individualization,
i.e. the declining social cohesion of Western society, has previously (chapter 11) been illustrated by time series of two indicators: the crime rate and the divorce rate. In figure 18.1. the
Western crime rate is reproduced and compared to that of Japan.
The difference is striking. While in the West the frequency has at
least trebled, Japan shows a virtually horizontal trend. True
enough, from 1973 onwards the frequency in Japan has also
increased slightly (from 74 in 1973 to 87 in 1982, 1957 = 100), but
this is nothing compared to the West.

The increase in Japan, however, is not without significance
considering the fact that youth criminality in particular is responsible for it. During the last decade Japanese youth has apparently
started to repudiate the choice-restricting conformism to traditional norms and values with an increasing crime rate as a spin-off.
In general, however, the graph justifies the assumption that the
individualization process in Japan – contrary to the West – has
only recently begun.

Figure 18.2. shows the pattern of the second indicator for the
same period: the divorce rate. The difference between Japan and
the West is comparable to the previous graph. In the West the
frequency has, once again, undergone a three- to six-fold increase, whereas Japan has only reached the level of 189 (1957 =
100). It should be noted that the relatively low increase in the
USA gives a somewhat distorted image due to the structurally
high number of divorces in 1957. Measured in absolute terms, the
USA in fact scores higher than all other countries. The difference
between Japan and the West is less pronounced than was the case
with the crime rate; in particular, during the last few years the
number of divorces in Japan shows a significant increase. This is
related to the changed attitude of Japanese women, who 'dis-
cover' their anomalous position (e.g. no lifetime employment,

Figure 18.1. Post-war crime rates in comparative perspective (crimes known to the police per 100,000 inhabitants, 1957–1984, 1957 = 100).

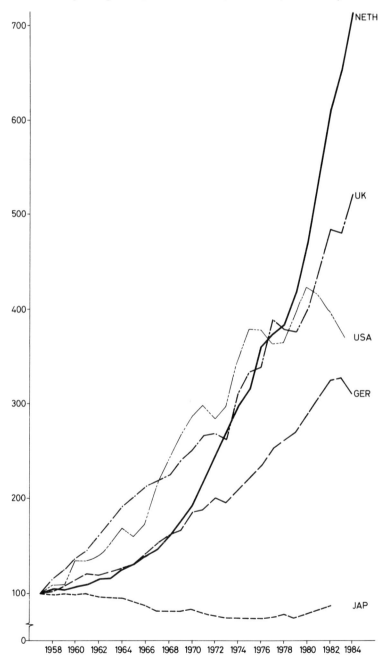

Source: See Appendix.

Figure 18.2. Post-war divorce rates in comparative perspective (per 100,000 inhabitants, 1957–1984, 1957 = 100).

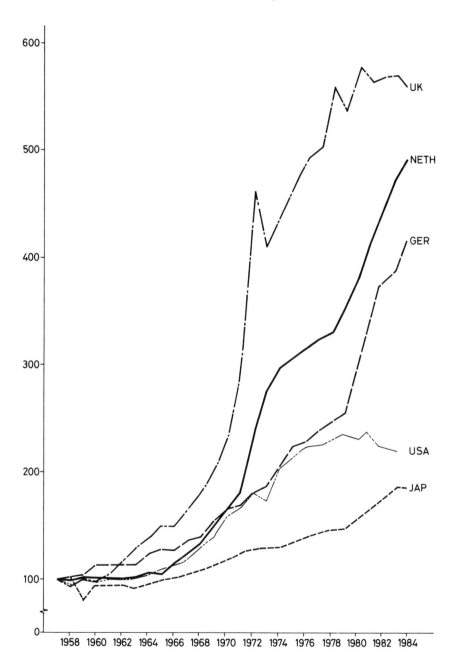

Source: See Appendix.

and in case of divorce little or no alimony) and try to follow a more emancipated way of life. This 'discovery' does not otherwise deny that – as was apparent from a recent international enquiry held by the Japanese government – the great majority of Japanese women, contrary to Western women, still believe 'that boys and girls must be brought up differently', 'that women should place not themselves but their husbands and family first', etc.

Summarizing, the different patterns of the indicators in Japan and the West confirm the specific characteristics of Japanese society pointed out by Nakane and Doi.

19. Western innovation

In a recent article by Peter Drucker entitled 'Behind Japan's success', the author quotes a friend who claims to be 'more afraid of the Japanese than the Russians (. . .). The Russians are clearly out to conquer the world, but their unity has been imposed from above and will therefore probably never survive a real challenge. The Japanese are also out to conquer, but their unity comes from inside. They act as a combined force which foreigners often refer to as Japan Ltd.'.[1] What Drucker means to say is that Japan's economic success can in particular be explained by the social cohesion of the country. Other factors, highly valued in the West as determinants of rapid economic growth, seem to play an insignificant role. Labour market mobility for example is low in Japan, at least in the world of big business where lifetime employment is normal practice. Furthermore, since wage differentiation is based on age, the Japanese worker seems to be little motivated by financial incentives. Even significantly rising wage levels have not damaged Japan's competitive strength. Like Nakane and Doi, Drucker points out that Japan's cultural characteristics – given the availability of Western technological knowledge – offer an ideal footing for a high growth rate. Individualization would work counter-productively in Japan.

In the West as well the individualization of workers has not as yet led to spectacular results, at least not in firms in which division of work (Taylorization and bureaucratization) has been pushed to the point that individual skills and creativity are hardly ever called upon. Unless – and this is our central position – Western firms pursue accelerated social innovation, i.e. change over to de-centralized control and smaller production units in which highly qualified and creative employees can more or less autonomously exploit the rapidly changing opportunities: unless these condi-

tions are fulfilled the rate of innovation in the economy will
remain below the rate realized by Japan. It is true to say that
Japan is also at the start of an individualization process comparable to that of the West. In the long run Japanese firms will
similarly have to adapt to this, as otherwise their prominent
position in the world economy will be endangered. Western firms,
however, have clearly failed to recognize the challenge of accelerated individualization in the last decades. The present situation
can probably best be characterized as an adaptation crisis in which
the institutions of the industrial age are increasingly becoming
obsolete, while new forms have not had sufficient time to crystall-
ize. (In the Appendix the relationship between the degree of
individualization and the economic growth rate is statistically
illustrated for the USA, Germany, the UK, The Netherlands, and
Japan in the period 1960–1984.)

The diagnosis is clear: individualism is not our weakness but our
strength.[2] It is a precondition for fully exploiting the opportunities
information technology is offering. Instead of gazing at Japan, we
should move ahead and utilize our comparative advantages. Accelerating the technological and social innovation of our firms
simultaneously will lead to a structural improvement of their
competitive, innovative, and self-regulating capacity. We want our
firms to stand on their own feet, instead of having to depend on
tariff barriers, government aid and other measures that distort
the market mechanism. Three global strategies are suggested by
the foregoing:

1. Formulated on an abstract level, each and every firm is con-
    fronted with the challenge of making a number of individual-
    ists work together, i.e. of creating an organization charac-
    terized by *integration with retention of individuality*. Such an
    integration is diametrically opposed to traditional organiza-
    tional forms where workers have a minimum degree of free-
    dom. In order to realize this new version, and to benefit from
    its competitive advantages, the following changes are neces-
    sary:
    – An individualistic attitude to work is evidently incompata-
      ble with short, cyclical, routine work. Reintegration of

work is necessary in order to both satisfy and utilize the drive for self actualization. A further precondition is a simultaneous rise in autonomy, i.e. a reintegration of control and performance. Self control, instead of top-down control, allows creativity to develop and serve the innovative capacity of the firm. Our human resources are becoming our most valuable asset. Comparative advantages are no longer based on technical knowledge (which has ceased to respect national boundaries), nor on the availability of venture capital (which is also international), but on the quality and utilization of one's working force.

– Integration with retention of individuality can only be achieved when the number of workers involved is limited. In larger firms a collective conscience needs to be artificially cultivated in order to maintain a high level of integration. Company ties, uniforms, and similar group symbols will then have to be used. For the new kind of integration, scale reduction, or dividing large companies up into smaller autonomous units, is therefore a prerequisite. Some companies (Philips in the Netherlands for example) seem to be aware of this and plan to split up and decentralize control. Their number is still small but unmistakably increasing. We are on the right track. The trendshift with the industrial past should, however, be drastically accelerated.

2. The second strategy derives from the specific characteristics of information technology. As explained in Part III this technology is eminently suited to reverse the historical trend of fragmentation and bureaucratization of work. Thanks to information technology, social and technological innovation can be simultaneously implemented, assuming that management is wise enough to replace conventional wisdom by more enlightened insights. Market forces in fact leave them no choice, at least not in the long run. The increased turbulence in the environment of the firm demands far more flexibility than traditional firms can muster.

3. The third directive follows on from the preceding two and concerns the necessity of 'life-long' education. Due to the

accelerated rate of technological change, knowledge ages rapidly, in any case, at least more than once per career. The information age therefore demands a high degree of cognitive mobility: the ability to rapidly assimilate new and diverse information. Life-long identification with certain knowledge, skills, or profession should be replaced by a more flexible orientation. The increasing information overload confronts the worker with an additional problem of choice. Much more than in the past he will have to rely on his own judgement: not only when he has to solve a problem, but also, and at least equally important, when he defines it. More generally, work in the information age requires specialists who are also generalists. Summarizing, the information age will require considerable innovations in our educational system. Skills should be continually updated during a career by a large variety of courses and practical training. In the preliminary training an important place will have to be given to the development of cognitive mobility, flexibility, and the ability to handle information overload. The additional courses should cover a system of life-long education, of continuous re- and post-schooling. The technical infrastructure (open universities, educational computer networks, and more generally 'schools without walls') and the expected further decline of actual working hours will allow this system to develop. As a result, the conditions will be created for the kind of human resource management under which the Western Edge will have an optimal chance to materialize.

20. Leading-edge pioneers

Nowhere is Taylorism and organizational complexity more evident than in the automobile industry. Within this industry the largest company, General Motors, has probably gone further in this respect than any of its competitors. One of Detroit's little jokes used to be that Chrysler's biggest asset was the complexity and resulting confusion of General Motors. GM was considered to be too big to move quickly in any direction whatsoever. Moved to act by fierce Japanese competition, Chief Executive Roger Smith in 1980 asked McKinsey to report on the relative position of GM in the world market. The results were shocking. While Toyota needed only 38 manhours to produce a car, it took GM no less than 144 hours. The alarm bell was rung; immediate action had to be taken to preserve the automobile industry as a vital part of the US economy.

GM's attempt to regain a competitive edge is exemplified by the ambitious 5 billion dollar 'Saturn' project in Spring Hill, Tennessee. The project is meant to be more than a show case solution of GM's internal communication and dataprocessing problems. Major organizational changes will be made, simultaneously eliminating layers of management and reintegrating work on the assembly floor. By 1990 the Saturn 'car of the future' is to beat the Asian imports that have been flooding the US market.

In June 1982, GM employees set out to create the Saturn plan from scratch. The Saturn car itself will probably look and drive much like automobiles today. More important than the product is the way it will be made. Virtually every aspect of traditional car making will be changed. Computers will be on center stage at every step. Labor relations will be radically different. The moving assembly line, a hall-mark of the automobile industry ever since Henry Ford, will be abandoned. Instead, cars will be made in a modular fashion. Separate teams of workers – 'work units' – will put together sections of the cars, such as the cooling system and the front-end unit (bumper, grill, radiator and headlamp, etc.). Each of these sections will be installed in a single step. Every member of the work-units will do a wide variety of work. Saturn will have no more than six job categories instead of the dozens of rigid job classifications in the existing plants. The pace of most jobs will be controlled by the workers themselves.

Saturn's workers are meant to be full partners. Representatives of the United Auto Workers will sit in on all planning and operating committees. To emphasize the new equality, blue-collar workers will earn a salary, just like managers. Both will earn bonuses based on performance.

Like experimental teams already working in a few GM facilities, the Saturn units will be responsible for controlling variable costs and doing quality inspections. They will also maintain equipment, order supplies and set the relief and vacation schedules of their members. However, they will have more authority than that. If a team comes up with a better idea for a new piece of equipment, Saturn's finance and purchasing departments must respond. The experts can't shrug off suggestions as they tended to do in the past.

Similar work-units are to be combined into work-unit modules. These will consist of up to six units; an 'advisor' will be assigned to each module to act as liason with company experts in engineering, marketing, personnel and the like. Work-unit advisors will also be a channel for information to and from the business unit: the committee that will manage the entire plant. This committee will include the plant manager, probably with another title, plus one elected UAW representative.

Saturn operations will be run by the 'Manufacturing Advisory Committee'. This committee will consist of top UAW and company officials from the business unit, plus the manager of the Saturn complex and an elected UAW official. It is supposed to decide on changes in salaries and benefits and will report on this and other decisions to the 'Strategic Advisory Committee', the highest level of Saturn management. Made up of a top UAW official plus Saturn's president and staff, this committee will handle long-term planning for the company.

One of the most remarkable differences with the traditional car factory is the sharp decrease in the number of hierarchical levels, illustrated in figure 20.1. In the traditional setting, one could distinguish at least eight: worker, supervisor/foreman, general supervisor, production superintendent, general superintendent, production manager, plant manager, and the board of directors. Saturn will have only four: work-units, business units, and the two advisory committees. This reduction is of course related to the no less remarkable horizontal integration indicated earlier.

As already mentioned, the completely new organizational concept (in which the traditional worker/management distinctions are blurred) is possible due to advanced applications of information technology. An integrated computer network will coordinate Saturn from design to delivery, cutting out many papershuffling jobs. Buyers can choose colors and optional equipment, arrange

Figure 20.1. Number of hierarchical levels in the traditional General Motors factory and in the GM-Saturn project.

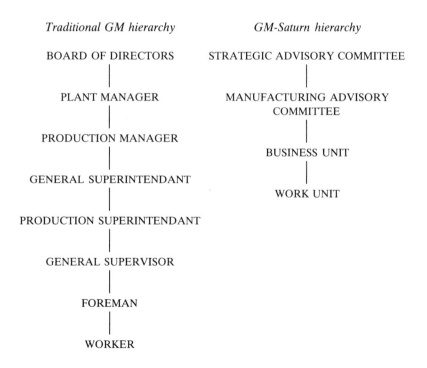

credit and financing and get a delivery date – all from a terminal at a dealership. Computers will convert customer orders into parts orders and production schedules. Each work unit has a personal computer providing information on their part of the job. The time from order to delivery could be as little as 12 days. The islands of automation in the present GM factory will be integrated. Offices, dealerships and plants will be tied into a smooth-working whole. By replacing the assembly line with a fully computerized production system that extends from the dealer to the factory floor, GM is betting that it can close the estimated $2,000 per unit gap between its production costs and those of its Japanese competitors.

To summarize, it would appear that Saturn is an excellent illustration of the trendshift from the past noticed in previous chapters. Work and management in the Saturn plant show very little similarity with the industrial past. The project may be conceived of as an exercise in the de-Taylorization, de-hierarchization and de-bureaucratization of America's largest companies exploiting the possibilities offered by information technology.

GM is an example from the industrial sector. For banks, insurance companies, and the non-commercial service sector, including the government, similar opportunities exist, especially now that computer networks and (increasing) intelligent, multi-functional work stations are available. Of the many successful examples we have selected the Dutch insurance company 'Centraal Beheer' (CB), particularly its motorcar department (CBM). CB is one of the largest insurance companies in the Netherlands with more than 2,000 employees. CBM seized upon the opportunities afforded by information technology to introduce major social-organizational innovation in the company. Until the late 1950s when the first computer was introduced, CBM was organized along traditional 'factory' lines. The organizational chart in figure 20.2. shows how the division of work had shaped the company's structure. Departments had been created around separate parts of the production process, such as 'acceptance', 'administration', 'damage inspection', etc. The shortcomings of this arrangement were revealed in the process of automation. Early computer applications were based on batch processing: each department in

Figure 20.2. Organizational chart of the Motor car department of the Dutch insurance company 'Centraal Beheer' before and after automation.

Before automation (1965)

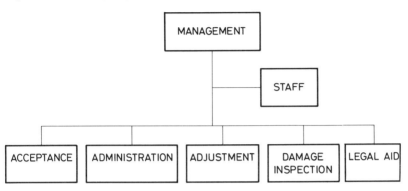

After automation (1985)

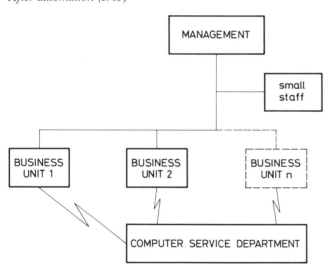

turn had to submit jobs to the computer center and wait for the results. This intensified the problems of coordination, particularly when computer breakdowns interrupted the flow of work from one department to another.

In the era of batch-processing it was not possible to communicate with the computer from one's desk. For this reason mistakes and breakdowns in the computer center usually had disastrous effects. The mediation of the computer broke the previously 'natural' link between sequential steps. The company's management at first tried to solve these problems traditionally by further specialization and simplification of tasks. Subdepartments were created to control the computer-input, planning, and output. Additional staff units were formed to handle the more specific cases. However, this previously adequate solution for the coordination and control of the production process now turned against itself. In particular, the need for marketing to adapt to changing customer requirements and new products could not be met properly.

Fortunately, information technology offered new instruments to cope with these problems. Microcomputers and work stations linked to the mainframe placed sophisticated computer facilities at one's fingertips. Batch processing was replaced by interactive communication with the mainframe from any place you wanted. Instead of having to carry information (the client dossier) from one department to another and process it in separate locations, all separate activities concerning an insurance contract could now be handled from one and the same place. A whole new structure for the company now became feasible.

Before automation	*After automation*
– separate departments responsible for a (functional) part of the production process	– self-contained units responsible for the whole product, i.e. a share of the market
– departmental employees all do the same monotonous work	– less division of work, more variety
– more specialists	– more generalists
– coordination at the expense of excessive central control	– coordination with/through local autonomy

Figure 20.2. also shows CBM's new organizational chart. The centralized, functional structure has been turned into a de-

centralized, divisionalized structure. Employees from different departments have been reallocated over divisions that are responsible for the whole product. Work is much more of a challenge; each division has a share of the market as if it were an autonomous firm. Desk-top microcomputers link every division to the mainframe; all desired information is readily available and processed on the spot. Furthermore, external communication has been integrated in the network. Major clients have terminals directly linked to the central computer. The ability to adapt quickly to changing customer needs has been dramatically improved. In addition to satisfied customers and more motivated employees, CBM's performance has been considerably upgraded. Simultaneous organizational and technological innovation has proved itself on the bottom-line.

CB and GM not only represent different industries, but different countries as well. Nevertheless their patterns of socio-technological innovation show some remarkable similarities from which a number of measuring rods for successful automation may be deduced. In fact, any Chief Executive Officer could find out whether his company is on the right automation track by answering each of the following five questions:
- Have I decentralized management responsibilities in the course of automation? Is the computer providing me all kinds of detailed information to control everything from the top or is it contributing to the self-control of more or less autonomous units at lower levels in the organization?
- Has the number of management layers in my company decreased? Has the computer contributed to the vertical integration of my company?
- Has the division of work and the number of horizontally linked departments decreased? Are my employees better off, not only in terms of compensation, but also in terms of the quality of work, i.e. has their work become more challenging? Has the computer contributed to the horizontal integration of my company?
- Has automation contributed to fine tuning production to the rapidly changing needs of the individual consumer? Has the company gained in flexibility and client-orientation?

– Has the productivity per manhour increased enough to bring down the size of my company in terms of the number of employees? (Unless your sales have risen tremendously, automation should – for better or worse – lead to reduction of your workforce.)

If you have answered yes to all five questions, you can be sure of one thing: you are capitalizing on 'The Western Edge'.

Notes

Chapter 2

1. Bell, D., *The Coming of the Post-Industrial Society: A Venture in Social Forecasting,* Basic Books, New York, 1973.
2. Netherlands Study Centre For Technology Trends, *Automation in the factory: starting point for policy,* Delft University Press, Delft, 1983, p. 2.
3. Porat, M.U., *Information Economy, Volume 1, Definition and Measurement,* U.S. Government Printing Office, Washington DC, 1977, p. 121.
4. OECD, *Information Activities, Electronics and Telecommunications Technologies,* ICCP 6, Paris, 1981, p. 29.
5. Little, A.D., *The Netherlands in the information age,* CIB, The Hague, 1982.

Chapter 3

1. Smith, A., *An Inquiry into the Nature and Causes of the Wealth of Nations,* edited by: Campbell, R.H., Skinner, A.S., Todd, W.B., Clarendon Press, Oxford, 1976 (1776).
2. Bücher, G., *The Genesis of the State Economy* (transl. H.), 1893.
3. Smith, A., *op. cit.,* p. 782.
4. Taylor, F.W., Shop Management, in: *Scientific Management,* Harper & Brothers Publishers, New York and London, 1947 (1911), pp. 98–99.
5. Wernet, W., *On the boundary between craft and industry* (transl. H.), Institute for Craft Research, Münster, 1965, pp. 72, 73.
6. Ferguson, A., *History of Civil Society,* Edinburgh, 1767 (IV, i., ed. Forbes 182–3).

Chapter 4

1. See for example:
   Dongen, H.J. van, The impact of new technologies on social change, in: Huppes, T., Berting, J. (ed.), *Towards the information society* ... (transl. H.), Stenfert Kroese, Leiden/Antwerp, 1982, pp. 89–105.
2. Schumpeter, J.A., *Capitalism, Socialism and Democracy,* George Allen & Unwin, London, 1979 (1942).
3. OECD, *Microelectronics, productivity and employment,* ICCP 5, Paris, 1981.
4. *The Wall Street Journal,* December 1986.
5. Jonscher, C., *Information Resources and Economic Productivity,* Sloan School of Management (MIT), December 1983.

Chapter 5

1. Rothwell, R., Zegveld, W., *Innovations and the Small and Medium Sized Firm,* Frances Pinter Publishers, London, 1982, p. 254.

Chapter 6

1. Evans, J., The worker and the workplace, in: Friedrichs, G., Schaff, A., (ed.), *Microelectronics and Society,* Pergamon Press, Oxford, p. 159.
2. Huppes T., *A new craft elan: work and management in the information age* (transl. H.), Stenfert Kroese, Leiden, Antwerp, 1985.
3. Waerden, Th. van der, *Schooling and Technology* (transl. H.), Doctoral thesis, Technical University Delft, 29 March 1911, p. 39.
4. Touraine, A., *Workers and Technological Change* (transl. H.), Paris, 1965.
5. Blauner, R., *Alienation and Freedom,* The University of Chicago Press, Chicago and London, 1973 (1964).
6. Braverman, H., *Labor and monopoly capital,* Monthly Review Press, New York, London, 1974.
7. Kern, H., Schumann, M., *Industrial Work and the worker's conscience* (transl. H.), EVA, Frankfurt/Cologne, 1970.
8. Kern, H., Schumann, M., Work and social character: old and new contours, in: Matthes, J. (ed.), *Crisis in the workplace? Report of the 21 German Sociological Assembly* (transl. H.).
9. Sitter, L.U. de, *Towards new factories and offices* (transl. H.), Kluwer, Deventer, 1982, chap. 4, paragraph 4.10.
10. Mumford, E., Henshall, D., *A participative approach to computer systems design,* Associated Business Press, London, 1979.
11. Reich, R.B., *The next American frontier,* Times Books, New York, 1983, pp. 117–127, 129, 130, 135.
12. Spenner, K.I., Temporal changes in work content, in: *American Sociological Review,* 1979, vol. 44 (December), pp. 968–975.
13. Rumberger, R.W., The changing skill requirements of jobs in de U.S. economy, in: *Industrial and Labor Relations Review,* vol. 34, no. 4 (July 1981), pp. 578–590.
14. Conen, G.M.J., Huygen, F., Riesenwijk, The qualitative structure of employment in 1960, 1971 and 1977, in: *Economic Statistical Bulletin,* (transl. H.), Rotterdam, 27 April 1983, pp. 361–369.
15. Institute for Small Business, *The quality of work in small firms in the industrial and construction sector* (transl. H.), The Hague, 1981.
16. Drucker, P.F., *Technology, Management and Society,* New York, 1958, p. 81.
17. Netherlands Study Centre For Technology Trends, *Automation in the factory: starting point for policy* (transl. H.), Delft University Press, Delft, 1983, p. 18.
18. Noble, D.F., Social Choice in Machine Design: The Case of Automatically Controlled Machine Tools, a Challenge for Labor, in: *Politics & Society,* vol. 8, no. 3/4, 1978, pp. 313–347.
19. Alexander, K., Has progress a future?, in: *Futures,* December 1983, p. 450.

Chapter 7

1. Mumford, L., *Technics and Civilization,* Harcourt Brace Jovanovich, New York and London, 1963 (1934).
2. Veblen, T., *The Theory of the Leisure Class,* 1934, p. 191.

3. Galbraith, J.K., *The new industrial State,* Penguin Books Ltd, Harmondsworth, Middlesex, England, 1975 (1967).
4. Toffler, A., *Future Shock,* Pan Books, London and Sidney, 1970, pp. 136–143.
5. Braverman, H., *op. cit.,* 1974.
6. Kern, H., Schumann, M., *op. cit.,* 1970.
7. Weber, M., *The Protestant Ethic and the Spirit of Capitalism* (transl. H.), Tübingen, 1907.
8. See for example: Sitter, L.U. de, *op. cit.,* 1982, p. 36.
9. Jonge, J.A. de, *The industrialization of The Netherlands, 1850–1914* (transl. H.), p. 4.
10. OECD, ICCP 5, *op. cit.,* 1981.
11. Reich, R.B., *op. cit.,* 1983, chapter 7.
12. Sitter, L.U. de, *op. cit.,* 1982.
13. Toffler, A., *op. cit.,* 1970, pp. 136–143.

Chapter 8

1. Dertouzos, M.L., Individualized automation, in: Dertouzos, M.L. and Moses, J., (Eds.), *The computer Age: A Twenty Year view,* Cambridge (MA), MIT Press, 1979.

Chapter 9

1. Lamborghini, B., The Impact on the Enterprise, in: Friedrichs, G., and Schaff, A., *op. cit.,* 1982, p. 142.

Chapter 11

1. Durkheim, E., *De la division du travail social,* 1893.
2. Weber, M., *op. cit.,* 1907.
3. Beteille, A., *Social Inequality,* Penguin Books, 1969, pp. 365, 366.
4. Weber, M., *op. cit.,* 1907.
5. Toffler, A., *The Third Wave,* Pan Books Ltd, London, 1981, pp. 177, 178, 399, 400.
6. Toffler, A., *Future Shock,* Pan Books, London and Sidney, 1970.
7. Huppes, T., *Income Distribution and the Institutional Structure* (transl. H.), Stenfert Kroese, Leiden, 1977.

Chapter 12

1. OECD, *Interfutures. Facing the future. Mastering the probable and managing the unpredictable,* Paris, 1979.
2. Inglehart, R., *The Silent Revolution. Changing Values and Political Styles Among Western Publics,* Princeton University Press, Princeton, New Jersey, 1977.
3. Inglehart, R., *op. cit.,* 1977, pp. 69, 70.
4. OECD, *Policies for life at work,* Paris, 1977.
5. Scientific Council for Government Policy, *The distribution and quality of work* (transl. H.), Government Press, The Hague, 1977.
6. Scientific Council for Government Policy, *The next twenty-five years,* (transl. H.), Government Press, The Hague, 1977.
7. The quality of working life, in: *Social Indicators of Satisfaction in Work and Social order* (transl. H.), 53, Bonn, May 1974.

8. Andrisani, P.J. et al., *Work attitudes and labor market experience. Evidence from the national longitudinal surveys,* Praeger Publishers, New York, 1978.
9. Gardell, B., Reactions at work and their influence on non work activities: an analysis of a social problem in affluent societies, in: *Human Relations,* no. 29, 1976, pp. 885–904.
10. Huppes, T., *Social consequences of the 'chip'-technology* (transl. H.), Stenfert Kroese, Leiden/Antwerp, 1982, chapter 4.

Chapter 13

1. Taylor, F.W., *Scientific Management,* Harper & Brothers Publishers, New York and London, 1947 (1911).
2. Roethlisberger, F.J., Dickson, W.J., *Management and the Worker,* Harvard University Press, Cambridge, 1939.
3. Herzberg, F., Mausner, B., Snyderman, B., *The Motivation to work,* Wiley, New York, 1959.
4. Maslow, A.M., *Motivation and personality,* Harper-Row, New York, 1954.
5. Hertog, J.F. den, *Work Structuring* (transl. H.), Wolters-Noordhoff, Groningen, 1977.
6. McCrae, N., The coming entrepreneurial revolution, in: *The Economist,* December 25, 1976.
7. McCrae, N., Intrapreneurial now, in: *The Economist,* April 1982.
8. McCrae, N., *op. cit.,* 1976.

Chapter 14

1. OECD, *Computertechnologies and consumerinformation,* Paris, 1982, p. 11.
2. Weiss, E.B., *The rising hide of individual taste,* Doyle Dane Bernbach Inc., New York, 1963.
3. Toffler, A., *op. cit.,* 1981.

Chapter 15

1. Social Cultural Planningbureau, *Social Cultural Report 1982* (transl. H.), Government Press, The Hague, 1982, p. 57.
2. Gershuny, J.I., The informal economy, its role in post-industrial society, in: *Futures,* Feb. 1979, p. 14.
3. Feige, E.L., The UK's unobserved economy: a preliminary assessment, *The Journal of Economic Affairs,* July 1981.
4. Gershuny, J.I., *op. cit.,* 1979, pp. 3, 5.
5. *Ibid,* p. 13.
6. Burns, S., *Home inc., the hidden wealth and power of the American household,* New York, 1975, p. 76.
7. Miles, I., Work and non work, Europe in the 1980's and beyond, in: *Futures,* December 1983, pp. 430–440.
8. *The FAST Programme,* volume 1, Results and recommendations, Brussels, 1982.
9. A.D. Little Inc., *The Netherlands in the information age,* The Hague, 1980.
10. Toffler, A., *op. cit.,* 1981.
11. Gershuny, J.I., Post-Industrial society, the rise of the service economy, in: *Futures,* Feb. 1977, pp. 113, 114.

{ }{ }{ }{ }

Chapter 17

1. *Robots in Japan, flexibele automation in production* (transl. H.), Government Press, The Hague, 1981.

Chapter 18

1. Nakane, C., *Japanese Society,* Penguin Books Ltd, Harmondsworth, Middlesex, England, 1981 (1970).
2. Doi, T., *The anatomy of dependence,* Kodansha International Ltd, Tokyo, New York & San Francisco, 1981 (1971).
3. *Ibid,* p. 28.

Chapter 19

1. Drucker, P., Behind Japan's success, in: *Harvard Business Review,* 1981.
2. A similar position is held by J. Naisbitt and P. Aburdene in their recent *Re-inventing the corporation,* Warner Books, New York, 1985.

Appendix

Table 1. (belonging to figure 7.2.) The average size of the firm in the industrial sector in historical perspective (USA and UK: employees per establishment; The Netherlands and Germany: including the self employed).

	USA	Germany	UK	The Netherlands
1930	41.2		31.4	8.4
1935	43.4			
1950	46.7			10.9
51				
52		63.7		
53		67.0		
54	47.2	69.9		
1955		73.3		
56		76.4		
57		80.1		
58	52.8	81.0	83.9	
59		81.9		
1960		85.7		
61		85.9		
62		83.8		
63	54.5	82.7		18.2
64		83.1		
1965		83.8		
66		82.6		
67	62.1	79.2		
68		82.5	93.9	
69		86.6		
1970		89.4		28.3
71				29.3
72	59.2	87.9		
73		89.1		
74		86.4		

Table 1. (continued).

	USA	Germany	UK	The Netherlands
1975		82.7		
76			60.7	
77	54.4			
78			57.9	
79			56.8	
1980		81.2		
81				24.6
82	53.7			
83				24.5

USA:[a]   1930–1954 : US Bureau of the Census, *Historical Statistics of the United States, From colonial Times to 1957*

             1958–1982 : *Statistical Abstract*, div. volumes

Germany:[b]   1952–1981 : *Statistisches Jahrbuch für die BRD*, div. volumes

UK:[c]   1958   : Her Majesty's Stationary Office, *The Report on the census of production for 1958*, 1963

             other years: Central Statistical Office, *Annual Abstract of Statistics*, div. volumes

The Netherlands:[d] 1930 : CBS, *Vestigingen onderscheiden naar het aantal werkzame personen*, 1930

             1950   : CBS, *Bedrijfstelling 16 October 1950*

             1963   : CBS, *Bedrijfstelling 1963, deel 4, ondernemingen*

             1970–1971 : CBS, *Statistisch zakboek*, div. volumes
CBS, *Sociale Maandstatistiek*, div. volumes

             1981   : CBS, *Sociale Maandstatistiek*, div. volumes

             1983   : CBS, *Aantal ondernemingen naar activiteit, grootteklasse en rechtsvorm*, January 1983

a. For all years: the manufacturing sector: establishments with one or more employees. Prior to 1958: firms instead of establishments.
b. For all years: 'Verarbeitendes Gewerbe' including 'Bergbau'.
c. For all years: the manufacturing sector: establishments with one or more employees.
d. For the years 1930 and 1950: the industry sector minus construction. From 1963 firms instead of establishments. 1963: 'industry and craft' minus construction. Number of firms 1981: estimated by interpolation from the period 1971–1983. Number of the workforce 1983: the same as 1981.

Table 2. (belonging to figure 11.1.) The crime rate in historical perspective (crimes known to the police, (1) per 100,000 inhabitants, and (2) indexed (1960 = 100)).

	USA		Germany		UK		The Netherlands	
	(1)	(2)	(1)	(2)	(1)	(2)	(1)	(2)
1900			860	50	259[a]	15		
1910			848	50	271[b]	16		
1920					282[c]	16		
1930			1201	70				
31								
32					488	28		
33							564	50
34								
1935							591	52
36							600	53
37	1026	55					598	53
38							566	50
39							550	49
1940					640[d]	37		
47	1074	57						
1950					1094	63		
51					1255	72		
52					1220	70		
53			1195	70	1123	64		
54			1162	68	1030	59		
1955			1237	73	1040	60		
56			1318	77	1138	65		
57	1394	75	1484	87	1283	74	1051	93
58	1510	81	1508	88	1477	85	1094	97
59	1524	81	1587	93	1586	91	1083	96
1960	1870	100	1705	100	1742	100	1127	100
61	1883	101	1775	104	1878	108	1147	102
62	1958	105	1761	103	2064	118	1213	107
63	2111	113	1816	107	2254	129	1220	108
64	2338	125	1890	111	2463	141	1318	117
1965	2224	119	1942	114	2598	149	1362	121
66	2412	129	2108	124	2732	157	1467	130
67	2990	160	2286	134	2717	156	1546	137
68	3370	180	2394	140	2892	166	1682	149
69	3680	197	2475	145	2087	177	1849	164

Table 2. (continued).

	USA		Germany		UK		The Netherlands	
	(1)	(2)	(1)	(2)	(1)	(2)	(1)	(2)
1970	3985	213	2768	162	3221	185	2025	180
71	4165	223	2811	165	3409	196	2313	205
72	3961	212	2963	174	3448	198	2586	229
73	4154	222	2912	171	3372	194	2862	254
74	4850	259	3120	183	3994	229	3115	276
1975	5282	282	3324	195	4283	246	3292	292
76	5271	282	3475	204	4346	249	3783	336
77	5062	271	3768	221	5014	288	3936	349
78	5124	274	3884	228	4878	280	4042	359
79	5548	297	4040	237	4833	277	4384	389
1980	5931	317	4303	252	5119	294	4939	438
81	5841	312	4584	269	5630	323	5719	507
82	5586	299	4860	285	6226	357	6461	573
83	5159	276	4893	287	6177	355	6878	610
84			4570	268	6659	382	7527	668

a. 1902.   b. 1912.   c. 1922.   d. 1944.

USA: 1937, 1942 : US Bureau of the Census, *Historical Statistics of the United States, Colonial Times to 1970*

1957–1983 : 'Offences known to the police', in: *Statistical Abstracts,* div. volumes, property and violent crimes. In 1965 the registration changed drastically due to a a change in the law; previous years have been estimated by interpolation

Germany: 1900–1939 : 'Anträge auf Erlass von Strafbefehlen', in: *Statistisches Jahrbuch für das Deutsche Reich,* div. volumes

1953–1982 : 'Bekanntgewordene Straftaten', categories 2, 3, 4, 5, 6, 8, and 9 in: *Polizeiliche Kriminalstatistik 1982.* For the years 1953–1956 category 6 has been estimated

1983, 1984 : 'Bekanntgewordene Straftaten', categories 3, 4, 7, 9, 11, 16 and 17 in: *Polizeiliche Kriminalstatistik 1985*

UK: 1900–1984 : 'Crimes (Indictable offences) known to the police', in: His/Her Majesty's Stationary Office,

Judicial Statistics, England and Wales, Criminal Statistics, div. volumes. From 1979: 'Notifiable offences recorded by the police'

The Netherlands: 1933–1939 : 'Processen-verbaal per 100.000 inwoners' in: *Statistiek der Gemeenten, Serie C, no. 1 t/m 6,* div. volumes

1949–1956 : 'Crimes known to the police' in: CBS, *Tachtig jaren statistiek in tijdreeksen*

1957–1980 : 'Crimes known to the police' in: *Maandstatistiek Politie en Justitie,* div. volumes

1981–1984 : 'Crimes known to the police' in: CBS, *Statistisch Zakboek,* div. volumes

Table 3. (belonging to figure 11.2.) Divorce rate in historical perspective, (1) per 1000 inhabitants, (2) indexed (1960 = 100).

	USA		Germany		UK		The Netherlands	
	(1)	(2)	(1)	(2)	(1)	(2)	(1)	(2)
1900	0.7	32					0.11	22
1	0.8	37			0.02	4		
2	0.8	37						
3	0.8	37	0.17[a]	19				
4	0.8	37						
1905	0.8	37					0.14	29
6	0.9	41	0.20	23				
7	0.9	41	0.21[b]	24				
8	0.9	41						
9	0.9	41						
1910	0.9	41	0.23	26			0.15	31
11	1.0	46	0.25[c]	28	0.02	4		
12	1.0	46						
13	0.9	41						
14	1.0	46	0.26	30				
1915	1.0	46					0.18	37
16	1.1	50						
17	1.2	55						
18	1.1	50						
19	1.3	60						
1920	1.6	73					0.28	57
21	1.5	69			0.09	18		
22	1.4	64					0.28	57
23	1.5	69						
24	1.5	69					0.29	59
1925	1.5	69						
26	1.6	73	0.54	61			0.32	65
27	1.6	73						
28	1.7	78					0.35	71
29	1.7	78						
1930	1.6	73			0.09	18	0.36	73
31	1.5	69			0.09	18	0.38	78
32	1.3	60			0.09	18	0.36	73
33	1.3	60			0.10	20	0.35	71
34	1.6	73			0.10	20	0.35	71
1935	1.7	78			0.10	20	0.35	71
36	1.8	83			0.10	20	0.38	78
37	1.9	87			0.12	24	0.40	82
38	1.9	87	0.72	82	0.15	29	0.38	78
39	1.9	87			0.19	37	0.37	76

Table 3. (continued).

	USA		Germany		UK		The Netherlands	
	(1)	(2)	(1)	(2)	(1)	(2)	(1)	(2)
1940	2.0	92	0.75	85	0.18	35	0.33	67
1950	2.6	119			0.69	135	0.64	131
51	2.5	115			0.64	126	0.59	120
52	2.5	115			0.75	147	0.56	114
53	2.5	115			0.67	131	0.52	114
54	2.4	110			0.62	122	0.52	106
1955	2.3	106	0.85	97	0.59	116	0.51	104
56	2.3	106	0.81	92	0.57	112	0.51	104
57	2.25	103	0.77	88	0.52	102	0.48	98
58	2.11	97	0.79	90	0.49	96	0.47	96
59	2.25	103	0.80	91	0.52	102	0.49	100
1960	2.18	100	0.88	100	0.51	100	0.49	100
61	2.25	103	0.88	100	0.54	106	0.49	100
62	2.21	101	0.87	99	0.61	120	0.48	98
63	2.26	104	0.88	100	0.67	131	0.49	100
64	2.35	108	0.96	109	0.72	141	0.51	104
1965	2.47	113	0.99	113	0.78	153	0.50	102
66	2.54	117	0.98	111	0.78	153	0.55	112
67	2.63	121	1.05	119	0.88	173	0.59	120
68	2.91	133	1.08	123	0.93	182	0.64	131
69	3.15	144	1.19	135	1.04	204	0.71	145
1970	3.46	159	1.26	143	1.18	231	0.79	161
71	3.73	171	1.31	149	1.51	296	0.88	180
72	4.05	186	1.40	159	2.41	473	1.12	229
73	4.36	200	1.45	165	2.14	420	1.33	271
74	4.62	212	1.59	181	2.29	449	1.41	288
1975	4.82	221	1.73	197	2.43	477	1.47	300
76	5.02	230	1.76	200	2.56	502	1.52	310
77	5.07	233	(1.22)	209	2.61	512	1.56	318
78	5.17	236			2.92	573	1.59	324
79	5.30	243	(1.30)	224	2.80	549	1.70	347
1980	5.20	239	(1.56)	268	3.01	590	1.83	373
81	5.30	243	(1.78)	305	2.94	576	2.00	408
82	5.10	234	(1.92)	328	2.96	580	2.15	441
83	5.00	229	(1.98)	339	2.97	582	2.27	463
84			(2.14)	366	2.90	569	2.37	484

a. 1901–1905.   b. 1905–1909.   c. 1909–1913.

Further information with regards to table 3:

USA: 1900–1919 : *Statistical Abstract,* div. volumes
                    1920–1956 : US Bureau of the Census, *Historical Statistics of the United States, Colonial Times to 1970*
                    1957–1982 : *Statistical Abstract,* div. volumes
                    1983   : *USA Statistics in Brief, 1985, A Statistical Abstract Supplement*

Germany: 1903–1914 : *Statistisches Jahrbuch für das Deutsche Reich,* div. volumes
                    1926–1940 : Rheinstein, M., *Marriage Stability, Divorce and the Law,* Chicago/London, 1972
                    1957–1976 : United Nations, *Demographic Yearbook,* div. volumes
                    1977–1983 : *Statistisches Jahrbuch 1983 für die BRD.* In 1977 the registration was drastically changed due to a change in the law; the statistics for the years 1977–1982 have been adjusted to link up with the previous years
                    1984   : Statistical Office of the European Communities, Eurostat, *Review 1975–1984,* Brussels/Luxembourg, 1986

UK (England   1900–1984 : Central Statistical Office, *Annual Abstract of Statistics,* div. volumes
and Wales):

The Netherlands: 1900–1956 : CBS, *Tachtig jaren statistiek in tijdreeksen*
                    1957–1980 : United Nations, *Demographic Yearbook,* div. volumes
                    1981–1984 : CBS, *Statistisch zakboek,* div. volumes

Table 4. (belonging to figure 11.3.) Tertiary schooling in historical perspective, (1) per 1000 inhabitants and (2) indexed (1960 = 100).

	USA		Germany		UK		The Netherlands	
	(1)	(2)	(1)	(2)	(1)	(2)	(1)	(2)
1900	3.13	18	0.86	23			0.61	17
1905	3.15	18	0.95	25			0.64	18
1910	3.84	22	1.09	29			0.70	20
1915	4.02	23	0.95	25			0.62	17
1920	5.62	32	1.96	51			0.83	23
1925	8.02[a]	45	1.43	37	1.25	52	1.28	36
1930	8.94	50	1.96	51	1.36	57	1.53	43
1935	9.43[b]	53	1.14	30	1.36	57	1.50	42
1940	11.28	63	0.71	19	0.91	38	1.17	33
1945	11.89	67			1.37	57	1.57	44
1950	17.46	98	2.34	61	2.03	85	2.94	83
1955	15.51	87	2.49	65	1.98	83	2.76	78
1960	17.80	100	3.82	100	2.39	100	3.55	100
1965	28.11	158	8.82	231	3.33	139	5.24	148
1970	36.79	207	11.08	290	8.21	344	13.47	379
71			12.54	328	8.44	353	14.49	408
72			13.60	356	8.60	360	14.94	421
73			14.86	389	8.81	369	15.31	431
74			15.95	418	8.82	369	15.81	445
1975	45.05	253	16.74	438	9.18	384	17.11	482
76			17.02	446	9.36	392	17.98	506
77	51.25	288	17.36	454	9.29	389	18.86	531
78	50.58	284	17.99	471	9.26	387	19.37	546
79	51.40	289	18.61	487	9.32	390	20.06	565
1980	53.13	298	19.67	515	9.50	397	20.21	569
81	53.79	302	21.27	557	9.86	413	20.27	571
82	53.49	301	22.58	591	10.08	422	20.81	586
83			23.75	622	10.31	431	21.37	602

a. 1926.   b. 1936.

USA: *1900–1970* : *US Bureau of the Census, Historical Statistics of the United States, Colonial Times to 1970*
                1976–1982 : *Statistical Abstract*, div. volumes

Germany: 1900–1960 : Mitchell, B.R., *European Historical Statistics, 1750–1970*, London, 1975 (students at universities only)
                1965–1983 : Statistical Office of the European Communities, Eurostat, *Education and Training, 1985*, Brussels/Luxembourg, 1986

UK: 1900–1983 : see Germany

The Netherlands: 1900–1983 : see Germany

Table 5. (belonging to figure 11.4.) Social security expenditure in historical perspective (in percentages of gross domestic product[a]).

	USA	Germany	UK	The Netherlands
1890	1.3			
1900				
1910				
13	1.2	5.4		
1920				
22				2.4
24			4.1	
1925				2.4
29			3.9	
1930	1.6			2.9
34			5.9	
1935	6.6			4.2
38				4.1
39			4.8	
1940	6.5			
1945	2.9			
48				6.0
49		11.7	9.1	
1950	6.4			6.2
52		14.5	9.8	
1955	5.7	14.9	9.3	6.4
58			10.4	
1960	6.8	15.4	10.8	11.1
1965	7.1	16.6	11.7	15.5
1970	9.6	17.0	13.8	20.0
1975	13.2	23.5	16.2	26.8
76	13.9	23.4	17.4	27.0
77	13.7	23.4	17.3	27.6
78	11.8	24.3	17.2	27.0
79	12.1	23.8	17.5	27.8
1980	12.7	23.8	17.7	28.6

| All countries: | 1960–1977 : ILO, *The cost of social security*, Geneva, 1981 |
| | 1978–1980 : ILO, *The cost of social security 1978–1980*, Geneva, 1985 |

USA   1900–1955 : US Bureau of the census, *Historical Statistics of the United States, Colonial Times to 1970*

Germany:[b]   1913   : Cipolla, C.M. (ed.), *The Fontana Economic History of Europe, Contemporary Economies-1*, Glasgow, 1976
               This concerns 'Social Services'
               1949–1955 : Wilensky, H.L., *The Welfare State and Equality*, Los Angeles, 1975

UK:[b]   1924–1939 : Mitchell, B.R., *Abstract of British Historical Statistics*, Cambridge, 1971
               1949–1958 : Wilensky, H.L., *op. cit.*, 1975

The Netherlands: 1922–1959 : Huppes, T., *Inkomensverdeling en institutionele structuur*, Leiden, 1977

a. The Netherlands: 1922–1959: national income; USA: 1900–1955: gross domestic product; West Germany: 1913: gross domestic product; UK: 1924–1939: national income.
b. The statistics from Wilensky have been adapted to the ILO-statistics.

Table 6. (belonging to figure 18.1.) The post war development of the crime rate in comparative perspective (crimes known to the police, (1) per 100,000 inhabitants and (2) indexed (1957 = 100)).

	USA		Germany		UK		The Netherlands		Japan	
	(1)	(2)	(1)	(2)	(1)	(2)	(1)	(2)	(1)	(2)
1957	1394	100	1484	100	1283	100	1051	100	1490	100
58	1510	108	1508	101	1477	115	1094	104	1480	99
59	1524	109	1587	107	1586	124	1083	103	1490	100
1960	1870	134	1705	115	1742	136	1127	107	1480	99
61	1883	135	1775	120	1878	146	1147	109	1490	100
62	1958	140	1761	119	2064	161	1213	115	1450	97
63	2111	151	1816	122	2254	176	1220	116	1430	96
64	2338	168	1890	127	2463	192	1318	125	1430	96
1965	2224	159	1942	131	2598	202	1362	130	1370	92
66	2412	173	2108	142	2732	213	1467	140	1310	88
67	2990	214	2286	154	2717	212	1546	147	1220	82
68	3370	242	2394	161	2892	225	1682	160	1220	82
69	3680	264	2475	167	3087	241	1849	176	1220	82
1970	3985	286	2768	186	3221	251	2025	193	1230	83
71	4165	299	2811	189	3409	266	2313	220	1180	79
72	3961	284	2963	200	3448	269	2586	246	1140	77
73	4154	298	2912	196	3372	263	2862	272	1100	74
74	4850	348	3120	210	3994	311	3115	296	1100	74
1975	5282	379	3324	224	4283	334	3292	313	1100	74
76	5271	378	3475	234	4346	339	3783	360	1100	74
77	5062	363	3768	254	5014	391	3936	374	1110	75
78	5124	368	3884	262	4878	380	4042	384	1160	78
79	5548	398	4040	272	4833	377	4384	417	1110	75
1980	5931	425	4303	290	5119	399	4939	470	1160	78
81	5841	419	4584	309	5630	439	5719	544	1240	83
82	5586	401	4860	327	6226	485	6461	615	1290	87
83	5159	370	4893	330	6177	481	6878	654		
84			4570	308	6659	519	7527	716		

USA, Germany, UK, The Netherlands: See table 2.

Japan: 1957–1982: National Police Agency, *Criminal Statistics*, 1982.

Table 7. (belonging to figure 18.2.) The post war development of the divorce rate in comparative perspective (divorces, (1) per 1000 inhabitants and (2) indexed (1957 = 100)).

	USA		Germany		UK		Japan		The Netherlands	
	(1)	(2)	(1)	(2)	(1)	(2)	(1)	(2)	(1)	(2)
1957	2.25	100	0.77	100	0.52	100	0.79	100	0.48	100
58	2.11	94	0.79	103	0.49	94	0.81	103	0.47	98
59	2.25	100	0.80	104	0.52	100	0.62	78	0.49	102
1960	2.18	97	0.88	114	0.51	98	0.74	94	0.49	102
61	2.25	100	0.88	114	0.54	104	0.74	94	0.49	102
62	2.21	99	0.87	113	0.61	117	0.75	95	0.48	100
63	2.26	101	0.88	114	0.67	129	0.73	92	0.49	102
64	2.35	104	0.96	125	0.72	138	0.75	95	0.51	106
1965	2.47	110	0.99	129	0.78	150	0.79	100	0.50	104
66	2.54	113	0.98	127	0.78	150	0.80	101	0.55	115
67	2.63	118	1.05	136	0.88	169	0.84	106	0.59	123
68	2.91	130	1.08	140	0.93	179	0.86	109	0.64	133
69	3.15	140	1.19	155	1.04	200	0.89	113	0.71	148
1970	3.46	158	1.26	164	1.18	227	0.93	118	0.79	165
71	3.73	166	1.31	170	1.51	290	0.99	125	0.88	183
72	4.05	180	1.40	182	2.41	463	1.02	129	1.12	233
73	4.36	173	1.45	188	2.14	412	1.04	132	1.33	277
74	4.62	205	1.59	206	2.29	440	1.04	132	1.41	296
1975	4.82	214	1.73	225	2.43	467	1.08	137	1.47	306
76	5.02	223	1.76	229	2.56	492	1.11	141	1.52	317
77	5.07	225	(1.22)	239	2.61	502	1.14	144	1.56	325
78	5.17	230			2.92	562	1.16	147	1.59	331
79	5.30	236	(1.30)	255	2.80	538	1.17	148	1.70	354
1980	5.20	231	(1.56)	306	3.01	579	1.22	154	1.83	381
81	5.30	236	(1.78)	349	2.94	565	1.31	166	2.00	417
82	5.10	227	(1.92)	376	2.96	569	1.39	176	2.16	450
83	5.00	222	(1.98)	388	2.97	571	1.50	190	2.27	473
84			(2.14)	419	2.90	558	1.49	189	2.37	494

USA, Germany, UK (England and Wales), The Netherlands: See table 3.

Japan: 1957–1979 : *Demographic Yearbook*, United Nations, div. volumes

1980–1984 : Statistical Office of the European Communities, Eurostat, *Review 1975–1984*, Brussels/Luxembourg, 1986

Individualization and economic growth in the USA, Germany,
UK, The Netherlands, and Japan in the period 1960–1984.

In chapter 19 it has been suggested that there is a relationship
between the individualization of society and diminishing economic growth (as long as we fail to exploit individualization by
way of social innovation of our firms).

In order to visualize the relationship, figure 1 shows the growth
rate in combination with an individualization index for four Western countries plus Japan (in total $5 \times 23 = 115$ points) for the
period 1960–1984. The growth rate is indicated by the percentage
economic growth per capita; the degree of individualism by the
average of the two indicators used earlier (the crime rate and the
divorce rate). The relationship per individual country is shown in
figure 2 (the averages of the variables for the periods 1960–1964,
1965–1969, 1970–1973, 1975–1979, 1980–1984). Both figures show
the same global picture: as the individualization index (on the
x-axis) increases, the economic growth per capita (on the y-axis)
declines. The relationship between the two variables is not linear,
but curved (with a correlation coefficient of 0.9). For each individual country, growth declines as individualization increases, as
is apparent from figure 6.2. The decline is most pronounced for
Japan. In the Atlantic countries the growth rate in Germany and
The Netherlands declined faster than in the USA, where, corre-
spondingly, individualization grew less rapidly. Finally the UK
shows the most horizontal course due to the low growth rate in the
1960s.

Of course the growth rate of a country is dependant on more than
just cultural factors. Research and development expenditures,
the availability of venture capital, the rate of technical innovation,
the size of the market, legal measures, exogenous factors such as
the oil crisis, the rise of Newly Industrialized Countries, all these
factors play their role as well. Moreover, the social indicators
could be criticized for their validity, international comparability,
etc. Nevertheless, despite these and other limitations, the variables show a surprisingly accurate relationship.

Figure 1. Individualization and economic growth rate in the USA, Germany, UK, The Netherlands and Japan in the years 1960–1984; see table 8.

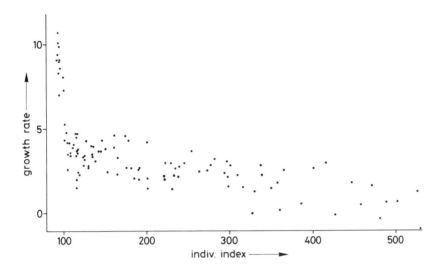

Figure 2. Individualization and economic growth rate in the USA, Germany, UK, The Netherlands and Japan in the periods 1960–1965, 1966–1970, 1971–1975, 1976–1980, 1981–1984; see table 9 (the dots for each country read from top left to bottom right show the chronological order).

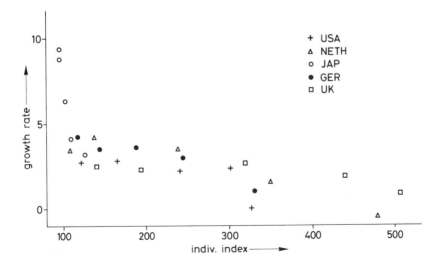

Table 8. (belonging to figure 1, Appendix) Individualization (1) and economic growth per capita (2) in the USA, Germany, UK, The Netherlands and Japan, 1960–1984.

	USA		Germany		UK		Japan		The Netherlands	
	(1)	(2)	(1)	(2)	(1)	(2)	(1)	(2)	(1)	(2)
1960	116	1.5	115	4.7	117	2.0	97	9.0	105	2.6
61	118	2.4	117	4.7	125	2.8	97	9.9	106	3.5
62	120	2.3	116	4.5	139	3.1	96	10.7	108	4.2
63	126	3.2	118	3.8	153	2.5	94	9.1	109	3.4
64	136	4.0	126	3.4	165	2.3	96	8.3	116	3.4
1965	135	3.5	130	2.7	176	2.7	96	7.0	117	3.7
66	143	3.7	135	3.4	182	2.7	95	9.4	128	4.3
67	166	3.3	145	3.7	191	2.0	94	9.1	135	4.0
68	186	2.1	151	3.8	202	2.1	96	10.1	147	4.3
69	202	1.5	161	3.9	221	2.2	98	8.6	162	4.6
1970	222	2.1	175	4.6	239	2.2	101	8.1	179	4.3
71	233	2.3	180	4.3	278	2.9	102	7.3	202	4.2
72	232	1.5	191	2.6	366	2.6	103	5.3	240	2.8
73	236	2.7	192	2.7	338	2.9	103	4.4	275	2.6
74	277		208		376		103		296	
1975	297	3.1	225	3.0	401	2.7	106	4.8	310	2.3
76	301	2.9	232	3.0	416	3.0	108	4.2	339	2.3
77	294	2.4	247	3.0	447	1.8	110	3.6	350	1.5
78	299	2.2		3.7	471	1.6	113	4.1	358	1.8
79	317	2.1	264	2.5	458	0.6	112	3.9	386	0.7
1980	328	0.5	298	1.7	489	0.6	116	3.5	426	0.0
81	328	0.2	329	1.4	502	0.6	125	3.1	481	− 0.3
82	314	1.1	352	1.1	527	0.7	132	3.1	533	− 0.3
83	296	1.4	359	1.3	526	2.2		3.0	564	0.0
84			364		539				605	

All countries: (1) The individualization index is the average of the index numbers for the crime and divorce rates, 1957 = 100 (see tables 6 and 7).

(2) 5-yearly moving average of real GDP per capita (year to year percentage changes) excluding 1974; 1984: 3-yearly average.

OECD, *Economic Outlook*, div. volumes (growth of real GDP at market prices less the population growth)
OECD, *Historical Statistics, 1960–1984*, Paris, 1986

Table 9. (deduced from table 8, belonging to figure 2, Appendix) Average individualization (1) and average economic growth per capita[a] (2) in the periods 1960–1964, 1965–1969, 1970–1973, 1975–1979, 1980–1984.

	USA		Germany		UK		Japan		The Netherlands	
	(1)	(2)	(1)	(2)	(1)	(2)	(1)	(2)	(1)	(2)
1960–1964	123	2.7	118	4.2	140	2.5	96	9.4	109	3.4
1965–1969	166	2.8	144	3.5	194	2.3	96	8.8	138	4.2
1970–1973	240	2.2	189	3.6	319	2.7	102	6.3	238	3.5
1975–1979	302	2.5	242	3.0	439	1.9	110	4.1	349	1.7
1980–1984	317	0.8	340	1.4	517	1.0	124	3.2	522	− 0.2

a. To neutralize the effects of the oil crisis, 1974 has been excluded.